Love to Aunty Em
on her hundred
from Flora

STARS ON SUNDAY

Peter Max-Wilson

PENTAGON

First published 1976

©Yorkshire Television Limited
A Member of the Trident Television Group

0 904288 09 9

Design by Brian Roll

Typeset, printed and bound
in Great Britain by
Butler & Tanner Ltd
Frome, Somerset

Acknowledgements

Stars On Sunday is a Yorkshire Television Programme

Producer
Peter Max-Wilson

Religious Advisors
Reverend Brandon Jackson
Monsignor Michael Buckley

Photographs
Brian Jeeves
Alan Harbour
Brian Cleasby

Extracts from New English Bible 2nd edition
ⓒ1970 by permission of Oxford and
Cambridge University Presses.

His Grace The Archbishop of Canterbury Dr Donald Coggan giving one of his talks on The Ten Commandments

The Archbishop of Canterbury
delivered the following talks

Talk One

Dr Coggan: Some people think that the ten commandments are 'old hat'. They are too negative for their liking—'don't do this' 'don't do that', 'don't do the other'. Well, negatives can be good for us. It's wise for a father to say to little Johnny 'don't touch the fire or you'll get burnt'. We'll be talking about these things in later programmes.

But tonight I'm going to read to you what Jesus said were the two commandments that matter more than anything else in life–they are positive enough, as you'll see. He was asked which commandment is first of all. His answer was 'Hear o Israel: the Lord our God is the only Lord, love the Lord your God with all your heart, with all your soul, with all your mind, with all your strength. The second is this: Love your neighbour as yourself. There is no other commandment greater than these.'

That is straight and clear. Love God, put Him first in your life. Love your neighbour whoever he is, respect him, care for him, as you show respect for yourself and as you care for yourself.

How's that for a rule of life? We would get a healthier society if we paid heed to that! And England would be a happier place.

What about beginning with you?

Talk Two

Dr Coggan: We've been talking in these programmes about the God who created us and who has given us certain rules for our healthy and happy living—we call them the ten commandments.

The one I'm going to read to you today *sounds* completely out of date—who of us has ever been tempted to make a graven image? As a matter of fact, it's up to date as tomorrow's newspaper. But first, let me read it to you.

> Thou shall not make unto thee any graven image, or any likeness of any thing that is in Heaven above, or that is in the Earth beneath, or that is in the water under the Earth: Thou shalt not bow down thyself to them, nor serve them: for I the Lord thy God am a jealous God, visiting the iniquity of the fathers upon the children unto the third and fourth generation of them that hate me; and shewing mercy unto thousands of them that love Me, and keep My commandments.

Well of course we don't make metal images and worship them. But we make *mental* images and worship them all right. Anything that's more important to me than God is an idol: a wrong ambition, a wrong relationship, enjoyment as the main goal of life, success as the be all and end all of everything. . . .

And what's all this about God visiting the sins of the fathers on the children. This is no picture of a vengeful God, wreaking his wrath on us unfortunate creatures. Not a bit of it. It is simply a statement of fact—that is you put yourself against the grain of the universe, if you break its laws, if you don't put God first, the results are to be found not only in your own troubled mind or diseased body, but in the minds and bodies of those who are in your family.

I believe we ought to see this commandment as a kind but deadly serious warning. God loves you and wants the best for you and your family. Put Him first.

Talk Three

Dr Coggan: Tonight's commandment in this series runs like this: 'Thou shalt not take the name of the Lord thy God in vain: for the Lord will not hold him guiltless that taketh his name in vain.' 'Don't swear. No bad language'—that's how this commandment is generally understood. We could do with a bit of a clean up here. The man who says 'bloody' in every other sentence shouts at us that he doesn't know how to express himself or to control himself; the book or play that is full of expletives— 'Jesus!' 'Christ!' 'My God'—makes many of us sick.

But this isn't really what this commandment is about. Actually it's a prohibition against making false promises. It's a command to keep your word. If you promise, perhaps on oath that you will do so and so, then you jolly well do it.

It used to be said that an Englishman's word is his bond. Is that true in your business? If not, the rot has begun right there.

When I lived in Bradford, my friends in the wool trade used to tell me that they didn't have written contracts. A word of agreement and a handshake, and the bargain was sealed. You don't go back on your word.

I say—Good for them! You can begin to build a healthy society along *these* lines.

Talk Four

Dr Coggan: Let me read to you a few words from Exodus 20 v 8–10a.

Remember the Sabbath Day, to keep it holy. Six days shalt thou labour, and do all thy work: But the seventh day is the Sabbath of the Lord thy God.

We Christians don't observe the Sabbath, that is to say the *seventh*, day of the week. We observe the *first*, because it was on the first day of the week that our Lord rose from the dead, and we want *specially* to remember Him on that day and to rejoice. The principle laid down in this commandment holds good for us all. We need a day on which to let up a bit. Not a day just for lazing but for re-creation. And if we're to be re-created, we must go back to the Creator, and think about Him—Who He is, what He has done for us and Christ, what He is willing to do for us, and in us, and through us by His Holy Spirit. *This means worship—* and that is the primary purpose of the first day of the week.

We can, of course, worship God in the open air. The question is: do we? We need to worship God in the company of His people, for there we hear the word of God, there we join in the sacrament, there we find the strength of fellowship one with another. What a travesty to think of Sunday as a dull drab day! It is the best day of the week, if you use it in re-creative activity, in renewal of body and mind and spirit.

Remember the Lord's day, and keep it holy. 'Christ is risen from the dead; set your mind on things that are above!'

Talk Five

Dr Coggan: The only story in the Gospels that we have about Jesus as a boy is the one that St Luke gives us in the second chapter of his Gospel—how He went up to Jerusalem with His parents and others, how they lost Him at the feast, and then found Him in the temple surrounded by the teachers, listening to them and putting questions to them with all the eagerness and curiosity of a twelve year old. The story adds that, after the expedition, 'He went back with them to Nazareth, and continued to be under their authority.' In fact, He observed the fifth commandment—'He *honoured* His father and His mother.' Let me read to you what He did at the *end* of His life. He is on the Cross. Nearby stands His mother and her sister and Mary Magdaline.

John 19 v 26–27 (N.E.B.)

Jesus saw his mother, with the disciple whom He loved standing beside her. He said to her, 'Mother, there is your son'; and to the disciple, 'There is your mother'; and from that moment the disciple took her into his home.

That was how He *honoured* His mother. This commandment—'honour your father and your mother'—has a word not only for the young but also for the middle-aged; old people constitute an increasing proportion of our population. Care for them is increasingly important. We must find more places where they can live with interest and comfort, and where they can die in dignity and peace.

Many of us ought to think again before we consign them to homes other than our own. The Africans have a lot to teach us here—with their strong sense of the clan, their respect for the wisdom of the old, their ability to hold together young, middle-aged and old in one tightly-knit community. We can learn from them, from this old commandment, and above all from Jesus Himself, to honour the old folk.

Talk Six

Dr Coggan: 'Thou shalt do no murder.' Well, I'm O.K. on that commandment. I've never killed anybody and I'm not very likely to. I may have come a cropper on some of the other commandments, but not on that one, thank goodness! Yes, but wait a minute, and listen to this. Here's Jesus Christ speaking to his friends:

Matthew 5 v 21–24 (N.E.B.)

You have learned that our fore-fathers were told, 'Do not commit murder; anyone who commits murder must be brought to judgement.' But what I tell you is this: anyone who nurses anger against his brother must be brought to judgement. If he abuses his brother he must answer for it to the court; if he sneers at him he will have to answer for it in the fires of hell. If, when you are bringing your gift to the altar, you suddenly remember that your brother has a grievance against you, leave your gift where it is before the altar. First go and make your peace with your brother, and only then come back and offer your gift.

That's strong language. Jesus is saying that murder is a thing not just of the hand or the gun or the knife but of the *heart*. We have broken this commandment if we nurse anger against our brother, or if we despise him in our heart, or if we hate him.

'I'll never speak to so and so again'—have you heard someone say that? Sometimes people who consider themselves good churchgoers say that kind of thing. Jesus says, if I may paraphrase his words, 'If you are on the way to church and you remember you've got some bad relationship, someone you won't speak to, or someone you have a grudge against, give your churchgoing a miss, go and seek out that person and *then* with your heart at rest and having overcome (or sought to overcome) evil with good, back to church you go.'

How many people are sick—yes physically and nervously ill—because they have neglected this commandment. There's health and peace in obeying it.

Talk Seven

Dr Coggan: Listen to this marvellous story.

John 8 v 2b–11 (N.E.B.)

He had taken his seat and was engaged in teaching them when the doctors of the Law and the Pharisees brought in a woman detected in adultery. Making her stand out in the middle they said to Him, 'Master this woman was caught in the very act of adultery. In the law Moses has laid down that such women are to be stoned. What do you say about it?' They put the question as a test, hoping to frame a charge against Him. Jesus bent down and wrote with His finger on the ground. When they continued to press their question He sat up straight and said, 'That one of you who is faultless shall throw the first stone.' Then once again he bent down and wrote on the ground. When they heard what He said, one by one they went away, the eldest first; and Jesus was left alone, with the woman still standing there. Jesus again sat up and said to the woman, 'Where are they? Has no one condemned you?' 'No one, Sir,' she said. Jesus replied, 'No more do I. You may go; Do not sin again.'

I love that story for two reasons. First, it shows us the bluntness of Jesus. He doesn't condone what this poor woman has done. Adultery is sin, and Jesus says so plainly 'do not sin again'. He knew that sex is one of God's loveliest gifts to men and women. The sex act is a physical act, but it is much more. It is a sacrament—a sign of a deep love of a man for a woman, a woman for a man, and should be entered into only where there can be total commitment, surrender of the one to the other for always. 'Don't spoil this' says Jesus. Your bodies are temples of the Holy Spirit. He's very straight.

The other reason why I love that story is this: It shows the *mercy* of Jesus. Those 'doctors of the law' seem to have been a self-righteous lot. Maybe they hadn't committed adultery. Maybe some of them had, and not been caught. But there wasn't a grain of compassion for the poor woman whom they had caught. Jesus fastened on this lack of charity, of love and concern. *That* was sin too, sin of the mind and heart, perhaps worse than the woman's sin of the body. Probably she had never known real love. Jesus showed it to her. Isn't that great?

Talk Eight

Dr Coggan: 'You shall not steal.' We don't use the word steal much today, do we? More's the pity. We nick, or we pinch, or we lift, or—well—'it just fell off the back of a lorry'! When we do a bit of cheating on the stock-market, or defraud the customs people on the way home from the continent, or slip an extra article into our pocket at the super-market when they are not looking—well, 'that's not stealing. It's being clever. One up for us!' I think there's disaster for individuals and for nations along *those* lines. And isn't it a kind of stealing when 20% of the world's population has 80% of the world's foods? That's a fact of our time—and a grim one at that. From one point of view, bearing in mind that all the world's goods come to us from God, isn't there a measure of cheating on the part of the rich West when we leave millions to starve in the poor East?

St Paul got it right. Listen to these words of his, straight and to the point:—

Ephesians 4 v 28 and 32 (N.E.B.)

The thief must give up stealing, and instead work hard and honestly with his own hands, so that he may have something to share with the needy.

Be generous to one another, tender-hearted, forgiving one another as God in Christ forgave you.

Ephesians 5 v 5 and 8–10 (N.E.B.)

For be very sure of this: No one given to fornication or indecency, or the greed which makes an idol of gain, has any share in the Kingdom of Christ and of God.

For though you were once all darkness now as Christians you are light. Live like men who are at home in daylight, for where light is, there all goodness springs up, all justice and truth. Make sure what would have the Lord's approval.

Talk Nine

Dr Coggan: 'Thou shalt not bear false witness against thy neighbour.' That's the last but one of the ten commandments, and pretty clearly it conjures up the picture of a man in the witness box, during a law-court case. He's got a down on his next door neighbour who has been had up for speeding. 'I saw the accident,' he says. 'He must have been doing at least sixty.' He didn't see him. He hadn't a clue as to how he drove. But the false word serves to get him a heavy sentence. He has vented his spite on him. That's 'bearing false witness'.

But there's more to this brief commandment than this. 'My dear, I wouldn't for worlds tell a soul but you, but have you heard about Elsie? I never *did* think much of her, but the other day . . .' And so poor Elsie's character is torn to shreds, all because two people gossip about her. The rumour spreads, and soon it's taken as gospel truth, and Elsie wonders why everybody avoids her.

'You shall not bear false witness.' A negative command. Oh yes. But a necessary command!

Judas bore false witness against his Master, and sold Him for thirty pieces of silver. You remember the sequel?

Matthew 27 v 3–5 (N.E.B.)

When Judas the Traitor saw that Jesus had been condemned, he was seized with remorse, and returned the thirty silver pieces to the chief priests and elders. 'I have sinned,' he said; 'I have brought an innocent man to his death.' But they said, 'What is that to us? See to that yourself.' So he threw the money down in the temple and left them, and went and hanged himself.

I doubt whether *any* of us have been quite guiltless on this score of bearing false witness and engaging in gossip.

Lord, have mercy on us!

Talk Ten

Dr Coggan: 'You shall not covet your neighbour's house; you shall not covet your neighbour's wife, his slave, his slave-girl, his ox, his ass, or anything that belongs to him.'

How old-fashioned it all sounds! At least, some of it does. I *have* known people who have coveted their rich friend's house, and I've known plenty of people who have coveted somebody else's wife—and sometimes run off with her. But we don't have slaves and slave-girls, and most of us don't have oxen and asses today! In the old days, of course, these were the things which made up a man's wealth. So if, in place of 'his ox and his ass', we said 'his bank-balance or his car or his pictures', we shouldn't be far off the meaning.

What is this commandment *saying* to us? Surely this:

Make up your mind which is the more important, the verb to *have* or the verb to *be*; the size of your wage-packet, or the kind of character you are. Take a *long* look at that one, for, at the end of life (which is really a new beginning), you won't take your wealth with you, but you *will* take the character you have made.

Jesus told a story about this once. Let me read it to you:

Luke 12 v 16–21 (N.E.B.)

There was a rich man whose land yielded heavy crops. He debated with himself: 'What am I to do? I have not the space to store my produce. This is what I will do,' said he. 'I will put down my store-houses and build them bigger. I will collect in them all my corn and other goods, and then say to myself, 'Man you have plenty of good things laid by, enough for many years: take life easy, eat, drink, and enjoy yourself.' But God said to him, 'You fool, this very night you must surrender your life; you have made your money—who will get it now?' That is how it is with the man who amasses wealth for himself and remains a pauper in the sight of God.

The story makes you think, doesn't it?

That's why Jesus told it!

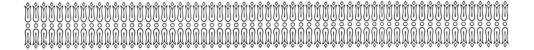

tars On Sunday began, from the audience's point of view, on Sunday 17 August 1969. For Yorkshire Television it began in early June of that same year. The Independent Television Companies supplied the music programmes for the religious, or closed period. Yorkshire's contribution in 1968 had been *Choirs On Sunday*, a format that provided for big choirs singing well-loved items from oratorios, operas and some of the best known hymns linked together by a well-known actor. The producer of this series had been Jess Yates and it was therefore natural that he should be asked to provide another music series this year for the six weeks that were Yorkshire's responsibility. His suggested format for these six weeks was an extension of the *Choirs On Sunday* idea but balanced in favour of the stars rather than the choirs.

He had felt for some time, that there should be a programme that was made especially for the older generations which would contain the sort of musical material that held a particular appeal to them. He drafted out the basic idea for an actual edition. It would consist of a male singer, female singer, choral item, song by child or children and a Bible reading and possibly an instrumental item. The programme would also include requests from the viewers and a presenter would read out the names and addresses of the people whose requests were included in the programme. Because the series would be only six weeks long a small nucleus of artistes was needed.

Harry Secombe, who was appearing at a theatre club near Leeds, was asked if he would be willing to take part. Maggie Fitzgibbon was in a play touring the country that was soon to be at the Grand Theatre Leeds. She was better known for her part in the series *The Newcomers* but had done a lot of singing in her native Australia. Both she and Harry agreed to appear in the new programme as did the Scottish soprano Moira Anderson who was in a summer season at Blackpool. The children for the programme were found in *Junior Showtime*, another series that Jess Yates was making. From there came young Glyn Poole and the Poole Family and Phillip Watkins. The obvious choices for Bible readers were Sir John Gielgud and Sir Ralph Richardson. Both theatre Knights were willing and able to take part. The choral item could be borrowed from last year's *Choirs On Sunday*.

By early August the first programme was complete apart from the all important position of the presenter. The choice fell upon a young lady already working for Yorkshire Television on the local magazine and news programme, *Calendar*—this was Liz Fox. It was decided to present the performers in the setting of a country house rather than the impersonal feel that a plain back-cloth setting tends to give. Some of the sets from the weekly series *Castlehaven* were borrowed for this.

During the week leading up to Sunday 17 August the first programme was edited together and at 7.00 pm Liz Fox presented *Stars On Sunday* edition 1. By 7.25 pm it was all over. Now came the wait to see if the programme was successful or not. By first post on Tuesday morning hundreds of letters had arrived in the office asking for requests to be played and complimenting the makers of the programme. *Stars On Sunday* edition 1 was a success.

The six weeks that *Stars On Sunday* was supposed to run for would be completed by September and the plan was for it to be replaced by another series of music programmes from one of the other ITV companies. But something happened during those six weeks that was to cause the programme planners to alter their schedules. What happened was not dramatic but it was so positive that it could not be ignored. When that first programme was transmitted on August 17 the audience figures showed that about $4\frac{1}{2}$ million people had watched. This was quite an increase over the size of audience that usually watched television at 7 o'clock on an August Sunday. The second edition increased the audience by about 2 million and the third did the same. By September 14, edition

5, the number of people switching their sets on to watch *Stars On Sunday* had risen to 10 million.

The letters for requests on the programme were pouring in by the hundreds each day and the programme planners realised that there would be a storm of protest if it was taken off. The public had demonstrated just how successful the format was simply by watching it. Throughout the length and breadth of the British Isles on those warm, still light, September evenings over 10 million people were coming in from their gardens or from a day's outing and switching on their television to sit down and watch a religious programme. It was these viewers that made the planners change their minds about finishing the programme on September 21.

Jess Yates was asked if he could cope with the run of the series being extended further into the Autumn. His answer was 'Yes, but I will need more studio time to be able to make it.' Yorkshire's studio schedules were rearranged to allow space for *Stars On Sunday* and that first series continued its run through till November 30.

Those first six programmes were made possible by the willingness of a small group of artistes to associate themselves with something new and untried. But for the series to continue new people had to be thought of and approached to take part in *Stars On Sunday*.

The Salvation Army had a group of singers known as the Joybelles. They were asked to appear in the programme and a long and happy association with the Salvation Army began. At the same time Adele Leigh was invited to sing for the viewers. Cliff Richard, who was equally popular with both the younger and older viewers, appeared on the programme on 5 October 1969 singing 'Reflections'. He was known for his views on religion and was a singer whose name had been mentioned in many of the viewers' requests.

That same month the home of *Stars On Sunday* grew a little bigger by acquiring a terrace and garden, which helped considerably in the presentation of the show. Another red letter day occurred for the programme on Sunday 2 November. It saw the first appearance of the Doncaster Wheatsheaf girls' choir, who were founded by John and Madge Barker and who were to be with the programme for a long time. Their youthful appearance and lovely singing was to help so much with the formation of the thousand-voice choir and other big choirs to be formed for *Stars On Sunday* in the future. What was particularly notable about November 2nd's programme was the first appearance of the film star James Mason, who was living in Switzerland and made only rare trips to England. During October and November 1969 he was on a visit to his father who lived in the Huddersfield area of Yorkshire. The format of *Stars On Sunday* was outlined to him and he agreed to appear. Since that time he has made over 50 appearances in the programme, a number that has been exceeded only by Harry Secombe who, to date, has made over 60 appearances in *Stars*.

By the end of the first series of 16 programmes more than 50 different songs had been presented by some 25 solo artistes and choirs. The three readers, Sir John Gielgud, Sir Ralph Richardson and James Mason, had shared between them the Bible extracts the viewers had requested. There was also one appearance in this series by Gerald Harper, who read part of the story of Zadok the Priest on October 12. So what had been learnt during that 16 week period? Perhaps the biggest lesson was that the programme had proved there was a very big audience who wanted to see and hear religious songs and readings presented in a tasteful and visually satisfying way. Ballads such as 'The Star Of Bethlehem' and 'The Lost Chord' had had their first airing on television and had been enjoyed by millions. Not that they were new songs, they had been favourites in Victorian times, but because, until now, there had not been a suitable programme for them to be played on, they were being heard by many for the first time. There were also many viewers who had loved and enjoyed them in their own childhood, so in a way the programme was helping to bridge the gap between the generations. It had been devised and created with the older viewer in mind but it had also attracted a big audience in the younger age range. What had to be done now, during the three months rest period the programme was going to have, was to sort through the thousands of letters that had arrived throughout the sixteen weeks and see if the artistes who were being requested could be persuaded to appear in the new series.

Jess Yates, the creator of Stars On Sunday

Harry Secombe

Moira Anderson

The Poole Family Tree

Sir John Gielgud

Liz Fox, Stars On Sunday's original Presenter

Gerald Harper

Stars on Sunday

Series 2 of *Stars* was scheduled to return on Sunday 8 March 1970. It had been decided that the successful format of the first series should be retained. What was different was the knowledge that 39 programmes were wanted. An enormous number of songs and artistes would be needed, in fact over 250 different items would be used by the end of it.

Liz Fox would continue as the presenter for the first 10 programmes. This would mean that she would have presented 26 programmes and her services were increasingly in demand for *Calendar*. A replacement would have to be decided on, but not just yet.

The first programme had three new faces on it for the viewers. They were June Bronhill, Vince Hill and Violet Carson. At the time she appeared for *Stars On Sunday*, June was a leading soprano with the Sadler's Wells Opera. The song she opened the new series with was the beautiful 'Nuns Chorus'. Ranged up the staircase behind her was the Doncaster Wheatsheaf girls' choir, looking as if there were over 100 of them rather than 42, and the visually spectacular appearance of *Stars On Sunday* was born.

By the end of March 1970, it was apparent that the programme had not lost any of its previous popularity, in fact the size of the viewing audience was as high as it had been during the winter months. There is usually a marked fall in numbers of viewers once the clock goes on that hour and the evenings suddenly get longer. But this had not happened. *Stars* had started to attract the sort of loyal audience that is normally associated with a long running series. Possibly the reason for this was that the programme had such a direct personal approach—it made contact with the people watching. They felt that it was being made specially for them—as indeed it was. Something that the programme had tried never to lose sight of over the years is that although there are millions of people watching they are watching in small units of twos and threes and often on their own.

The first seven shows of this second series followed the same pattern as the earlier series excepting that on show 6 the viewers were introduced to a purely instrumental item. It was the Pontefract Caledonian Pipe Band looking splendid in their Highland costumes, with the drums rolling and the pipes singing out the lilting tune of 'Marie's Wedding'. This took place in the garden setting of the house and the response was very enthusiastic, judging from the letters. By this time the viewers were writing in not only for requests but to pass comment on each Sunday's programme. It seemed sometimes as if people were writing their letters whilst watching the programme, they arrived in the *Stars On Sunday* office so quickly.

Stars on Sunday

The edition transmitted on Sunday 26 April 1970 introduced another element into the programme. A new setting had been created especially for the ballerina Patricia Ruanne to dance an interpretation of the beautiful tune 'Meditation!' It was an old ruined abbey that was to be used on many occasions in the programme for dancers, soloists and choirs. It was to be very useful in a few weeks time when *Stars* made its only venture into the field of drama. On the same Sunday the popular American singer Gene Pitney made his first appearance.

May 10 saw two great ladies from totally different areas of the entertainment profession follow each other in that evening's programme. From the world of films and the theatre came Dame Anna Neagle to read from the Bible. Whilst from the variety theatre came the legendary Eartha Kitt. Miss Kitt did not sing that evening but recited the moving poem 'Morning Star' to a background of gentle organ music. The organist was the programme's producer, who played for nearly all the artistes who appeared on *Stars On Sunday*. At this time he was also directing the shows from the control box and writing the linking material for the presenter.

Apart from the first appearance on *Stars* of Dame Anna and Eartha Kitt, that edition also saw another presenter, Virginia Stride. On Virginia's final week, May 24 she introduced an excerpt, specially adapted for *Stars On Sunday* from Ronald Millar's new play *Abelard and Heloise*. The abbey setting was used for the performance, Keith Michel was Peter Abelard and Diana Rigg, Heloise. This was Keith Michel's second appearance on *Stars*. Three weeks previously on May 3 he had read from St Luke's Gospel chapter 11 verses 41 to 51 where Jesus reproves the Pharisees for being hypocrites.

The decision to include the play adaptation in the programme was a very big departure from the format that had become so popular over nearly forty weeks. There were only two solo singers in this edition—Matt Munro and Violet Carson—and it ended with Harry Secombe and a choir singing Handel's 'Largo'. It was a departure from the norm that was not really supported by the viewers. Whilst many of the letters received during the following week said that they thought it had been done very well, most of them showed that what they really wanted to see and hear was the mixture of solo songs, choral numbers and Bible readings that they were used to. As a result of these letters this pattern has hardly ever been changed since that time.

The following week, June 7, saw the lowest figures ever recorded for *Stars On Sunday*. Was it the public expressing their disappointment at the change from the usual format? No, it was not that at all, it was the

BBC transmitting the final of the World Cup football competition from Mexico. Obviously many of *Stars On Sunday*'s loyal viewers were also football fanatics. Fortunately it turned out to be just for that week. On June 14 which saw the first appearance of a clergyman in the programme, the viewers were back to the usual average of $10\frac{1}{2}$ million. The clergyman referred to was Dr Donald Coggan, at the time Archbishop of York now at Canterbury.

He read from the book of Isaiah chapter 55. It was the first time that someone other than a 'star name' had given the Bible reading. The viewers' response was overwhelmingly in favour of His Grace taking part in the programme.

They were also delighted by the first appearance that evening of a group of South American instrumentalists calling themselves Los Picaflores, consisting of three sisters and their brother. Although playing Paraguayan music and calling themselves by a Paraguayan name, they were British and were the children of a missionary father, Archdeacon Tony Barrett, who with his wife and family had served with the South American Missionary Society since 1952.

By this time Virginia had left the programme and Moira Lister had taken over presenting the artistes and introducing the requests. Moira was also only able to stay for a few weeks because of previous commitments but she was to return some years later. She was followed in turn by Alexandra Bastedo and Mary Holland.

July 1970 saw the first appearance in the programme of singing star Roy Orbison and film star Raymond Massey. The arrival of Roy Orbison, which coincided with that of Los Picaflores, saw the addition of a superb fountain consisting of four dolphins disgorging great cascades of water into a pool.

Around the back of the pool was a curved sloping walk, absolutely ideal for a big choir. The choir that sang in that setting was the 150-voiced Yorkshire Police choir. This choir was to join forces at a later date with others from all over the North of England and North Wales to form the enormous 1000-voiced choir that by early next year was to establish the tradition of closing the programme with a big choral number.

Even men require some make-up for colour television and on the visit of those 150 burly Yorkshire policemen to the *Stars On Sunday* set, it turned out, when we looked at them on the camera, that there was one who really needed to have some make-up put on. He was in the centre of the back row, a sergeant, about 20 stone and 6ft. 4ins. tall with a rapidly thinning head of silver hair. It was a combination of his size and the place where he was standing that caused the trouble. A light, which was very necessary for the look of the picture, was bouncing off his head and doing strange things to the overall shot. It looked as if a piece of the moon was part of the back row of this mass of blue uniforms, silver buttons and rugged faces. There was nothing for it—that head had to have some make-up powder put on it to cut down the glare.

Instructions were passed to the young make-up lady on the studio floor, who was every inch of 5ft. 2ins. She advanced, make-up tray in hand, upon the sea of blue serge. Every pair of eyes was on her—who was going to receive the treatment? It was quite an undertaking for her, picking her way slowly up the ramp towards the centre of the back row. She reached her destination and stopped. 'Do you mind bending forward?' she asked the by now red-faced sergeant. He did and quickly she dabbed the powder puff over the top of his head. A great cheer went up from the whole studio swiftly followed by a round of applause. The make-up lady beat a hurried retreat back down the ramp to relative anonymity behind the range of studio lights and cameras. The ripple of amusement the incident aroused settled down and the choir proceeded to sing some stirring tunes for inclusion in the programme.

August 1970 saw the appearance of the Bachelors, Norman Wisdom— as a singer—the young film star Hywel Bennett and the popular ballad singer Matt Munro. Matt was to sing his song, 'Sunrise Sunset', on the terrace setting that had just been introduced to the series. Part of this set was a lovely balustrade that curved gently round the edge of the terrace to the place where the steps led down into the garden.

He was half way through a rehearsal of the song when there was a sudden disturbance in one corner of the studio. Jess Yates was seen to be in heated discussion with a director from another studio along the corridor. The cause of this altercation appeared to be the balustrade that Matt was actually sitting on. What could be the problem? It soon became apparent that the said bit of balustrading did not belong to *Stars On Sunday* but to one of the settings for the new series of *The Main Chance*. It was actually part of the balcony outside David Main's suite of offices. Jess had, whilst walking through *The Main Chance* studio the previous evening, seen it and realised it was just what was needed to complete the terrace setting for *Stars On Sunday*. He had made some enquiries and been assured that the scenes that were due for shooting in that particular episode of *The Main Chance* did not involve anyone opening the French windows in David Main's office and showing the balcony. Accordingly he made arrangements for the balustrade to be moved into the *Stars* studio ready for Matt Munro the following morning.

Stars on Sunday

Unfortunately the person who had given Jess the necessary assurances had obviously failed to read the script properly for that particular episode. Scene 1 opens in David Main's office with Main sitting behind his desk. Almost immediately he gets up and goes to the French windows, opens them and steps out on to the balcony. Now as David Main's office was designed and shot to look as if it was on the eighth floor of an office block, when he opened the doors to go out to the balcony it looked for all the world to the startled director in the control room as though Main was about to take a suicidal leap out of the window. Great consternation, where was the balcony balustrading? Nobody seemed to know. The scenes crew was positive it had been in place the night before.

Now, in common with most television studios, Yorkshire has what is known as a house monitoring system whereby by pressing a given button you can see what is happening in the other studios that are working. The *Stars On Sunday* studio had been on one of the screens in the control room of the *Main Chance* studio but nobody had been paying the pictures any special attention until the loss of the balcony had become apparent. As the production crew for *The Main Chance* sat in their control room ruminating on the disappearance of one large piece of balcony the pleasing pictures from the *Stars On Sunday* studio began to hold their interest. That balustrade Matt Munro was sitting on bore a remarkable resemblance to the missing David Main balcony. Surely it could not be?

Well the only way to find out was to go into the *Stars* studio and take a closer look at it. Hence the discussion taking place in the corner during Matt's rendering of 'Sunrise Sunset'. A temporary compromise was reached. The song could be recorded with the balustrade but then it would be removed and returned once more to David Main's office. Within a matter of days *Stars On Sunday* had acquired its own gently curving balustrade which we still have today.

August saw two more lady presenters introducing the programme. Katie Boyle and Polly Elwes. It was also the month that saw Jess Yates appearing in the programme for the first time. This came about by pure chance. An artiste, whom we will not mention, had been engaged to present some editions of *Stars* and at the last minute had decided to go on holiday. Come the day for linking the programme together there was no one to do it. 'There is nothing else for it,' Jess said to his secretary, 'I'll have to do this one myself.' It was not really that big a jump because he had been writing the scripts for the introductions since the first programme. Now he was going to have to say them himself.

The programme was transmitted and, as was usual, the letters started pouring into the office from first thing Monday morning. They all, without exception, commented on the 'New Presenter'. He was the first and, until much later in the programme's life, the only man to introduce the show. This may well have had a lot to do with the obvious enthusiasm with which his appearance was greeted. As a result of the response from the viewers a meeting took place between the controller of programmes and Jess. At that meeting it was agreed that he should continue to introduce the programme—certainly for the time being. What this move did bring into question was the enormous amount of control over direction of the programme which was placed in one man's hands.

The Independent Broadcasting Authority which in those days was known as the Independent Television Authority, was approached and its views on the matter asked for. Among the dozen or so committees that give their advice, the two that relate to *Stars On Sunday* are the Central Religious Advisory Committee, known as CRAC, and the Panel of Religious Advisers. Both committees have representatives of the Anglican, Catholic, Methodist and Free Churches as members, so the advice comes from a good broad base. The IBA also has its own Religious Officer, who is in close touch with both the advisory committees and with the producers of ITV's religious programmes including *Stars On Sunday*. At this time in the programme's history it was Christopher Martin, who still holds this key position. Through Christopher the suggestion that Jess should become the programmes presenter as well as producer was put to the Religious Advisers and CRAC. It was agreed to but it was felt that, as *Stars* was obviously beginning to look like a long running series, the programme should carry its own religious advisers.

This decision heralded the arrival of two totally different clerical gentlemen. From the Ecumenical centre at Woodhall near Wetherby came the tall grey-haired figure of their Irish director. Quick talking, quick thinking and quick moving, Monsignor Michael Buckley, representing the Catholic church. Whilst from Shipley came the young forceful personality of the Vicar of St Peters, Brandon Jackson. Their arrival on the scene undoubtedly brought new strengths to the religious content of the programmes by introducing the idea of a theme for each week's group of artistes and songs. This long series of 39 editions continued its way through the summer and autumn of 1970.

Rolf Harris made his début towards the end of September and the pop singer Joe Brown appeared on October 4 singing 'All Things Bright and Beautiful' with a backing chorus made up of the Leeds Girls' Choir.

Later during October Andy Stewart and Edmund Hockeridge joined the ever swelling ranks of *Stars On Sunday*. November 8 saw *Stars On*

Stars on Sunday

Sunday's first special programme for Remembrance Day. The reading of Lawrence Binyon's moving poem 'For the Fallen' was undertaken by Gerald Harper and that edition closed with the Colne Valley Male Voice Choir's rendering of Comrades in Arms.

The following Sunday saw a very special high spot in the series. Miss Gracie Fields, who had been retired for some years and was living in the Isle of Capri with her husband Boris Apperevici, made her first appearance. An enormous amount of time and effort had been spent to achieve the two-and-a-half-minute appearance.

The idea was for Miss Fields to be flown over to the Leeds studios to record a special Christmas Day hour-long programme for transmission immediately prior to the Queen's Christmas Message to the nation. Whilst in Leeds for this special programme she would also sing some songs for inclusion in *Stars*.

She agreed to these suggestions and the recording day arrived. By co-incidence that day also happened to be her husband Boris' birthday. Unknown to either of them Yorkshire's canteen staff had baked a large birthday cake and during a break in the session the lights were dimmed and on to the set was wheeled the cake, all candles lit, to the tune of 'Happy Birthday' played by the programme's presenter/producer. Both of them had been having a quiet chat during the break and were taken completely unawares and then Gracie joined in the singing with the rest of the studio.

Two weeks after Miss Fields' first appearance, the film star Peter Sellers made another departure from the usual pattern by reading not from the Bible but a poem called 'Abu Ben Adham'.

The following Sunday, December 6 was the last one of the series and Vincent Price made his first appearance reading a letter first printed in a small town newspaper at the turn of the century. It was, in fact, the editor's answer to a question from a little girl who had written to the paper saying that she had been told there was no Santa Claus.

The programme was now due for a break but not a long one. The date had been set for the beginning of the new series which was to be 3 January 1971.

Virginia Stride

Andy Stewart

Patricia Ruanne

Keith Michel

Katie Boyle and Mary Holland
Presenters of Stars 1970

Moira Lister
Presenter of Stars 1970 and 1974

Matt Munro

Miss Violet Carson

Norman Wisdom

Eartha Kitt

Peter Sellers

Los Picaflores

Vincent Price

Miss Gracie Fields

Gene Pitney

Stars on Sunday

The Christmas break from transmission for *Stars On Sunday* was to be for only a brief period of three weeks. *Stars On Sunday* series 3 started on the first Sunday of the New Year with Jess Yates as the presenter and Katie Boyle co-presenting and was to run through to high summer.

The letters were continuing to flood in at around 2000 a week and it was becoming apparent that a great number of viewers were beginning to write to the programme as a friend. Most letters did not require an answer but some were clearly a call from people who lived a very lonely life and felt that *Stars On Sunday* was a point of contact. It has always been the policy of the programme not to ignore these letters but to reply to them. A secretary was appointed and an office set up which did nothing else but handle the viewers' correspondence. If a letter indicates that the sender needs a more specialised answer than the Producer is able to give, then it is passed on to one of the programme's religious advisers and they bring their expertise and knowledge to the reply. Since the first day of *Stars On Sunday* nearly half-a-million letters have arrived in the office.

It is an unfortunate fact that any one edition of *Stars On Sunday* can only accommodate between 25 and 30 dedications so there are always many writers who do not get their particular dedication read out. However, we do try to cover the whole country with a fair balance reflecting the areas from which the requests come. The programme has always tried to mark such important events in people's lives as anniversaries and birthdays, but we do need a few weeks advance notice.

As you might expect, with a programme that invites viewers to write to it, we do sometimes get some very strange letters. Most of the weird ones tend to be sent by people who appear to have strange hang-ups about religion—that is all forms of religion except for their own personally worked-out road to salvation. These letters are also passed on to the programme's religious advisers. The other type of letter writer, who is out of the usual, is the highly abusive and rude sort who invariably makes personal and derogatory attacks on either the artistes taking part in the programme or the presenter. Almost without exception this type of person does not have the courage to put their name or address on the letter and they consequently go straight into the wastepaper-basket, more often than not without even being read. If you, for a moment, imagine *Stars On Sunday* as something that is living—then the letters work in the same sort of way as the human pulse beat. They give a very good indication of how the viewing public feel about the programme.

January gave way to February without any new stars making their first appearances in the programme but the series was maintaining the high level of artistes that the preceding one had done. During those first few weeks of the New Year the programme included such names as: James Mason, Gracie Fields, Vincent Price, Dame Anna Neagle, Raymond Massey, Harry Secombe, Violet Carson, Norman Wisdom, Maggie Fitzgibbon, John Hanson, June Bronhill, Rolf Harris, The Bachelors, Andy Stewart plus the Archbishop of York and many choirs both large and small.

Amongst the large choirs was the Salvation Army massed choirs and bands under their conductor Brigadier Brindley Boon. The setting that was used for them was an adaptation of the enormous ballroom that had been created for 'A Gift for Gracie'. Ranged up the stairs were over 200 uniformed Salvationist songsters whilst along the windowed wall the band of 50 instrumentalists was set out. The items recorded were typical of the Salvation Army's approach to their work, full of joy and hope.

In early February Tom Springfield came to the studios to record a new song for *Stars*. It was based on the moving prayer of St Francis of Assisi, entitled 'Lord make me an Instrument of Thy Peace', and over the succeeding five years it has been sung by many different guests to the programme.

In March Johnny Mathis made his début with the appropriately entitled song 'If we only had love'. March saw another innovation to the programme, the singing voice of *Junior Showtime*'s likeable young presenter Bobby Bennett. With him came the paddock setting and the songs of the pioneer west that were to prove so popular with the viewers. *Stars On Sunday* had opened up another area of music that had not been heard on British television—the old time religious music that had sustained the settlers who had created the Western States of America. The musical content of the programme was now becoming all embracing. The settings were fairly evenly balanced between interior and exterior and the new paddock had made possible the introduction of animals into the programme, which, as the producer maintained are also part of God's world. Accompanying Bobby that night were the Young Ladies of *Stars On Sunday* who were, with a few changes in their ranks, to continue with the programme through to today.

In April Noel Harrison made his début as did Anita Harris and Barry Kent both of whom are still regular guests on the programme. During that month *Stars* also saw the first appearance of the 100 parish choirboys in their scarlet cassocks with their lighted candles. Harry Secombe was joined by them for some of his appearances. The setting was the old ruined abbey and it had been decided to import some sheep to have gently grazing around the fringes of the abbey.

Unfortunately the specially selected sheep had two major drawbacks, they knew nothing about television productions and therefore behaved with what seemed like lunatic energy as they leaped all over the setting instead of gently grazing, and they had somehow neglected to become house-trained so choirboys and Mr Secombe had to tread with extreme caution. Despite these hazards to good singing, the final results were very pleasing both visually and musically. It is a day that one suspects Harry Secombe may still well remember.

Early May was marked by the appearance of American singing star Howard Keel. It was his first time in the Yorkshire Television studios, although he has returned since that occasion, and it was interesting to notice the way Yorkshire Television personnel kept finding reasons to pop into the *Stars On Sunday* studio.

The following week saw the appearance of Lovelace Watkins. He had been seen by the programme's producer singing in a club in Liverpool and had made a big impression with the power of his performance.

The week after Lovelace's first appearance saw two more new faces for the programme's viewers, Max Bygraves and Stuart Damon who had co-starred with Alexandra Bastedo in the successful series *The Champions*.

Ronnie Hilton and Sandie Shaw also made their débuts during the course of this series as did the very popular violinist Max Jaffa. His appearance saw the introduction of 'the quiet moment' to the programme. The purpose of this quiet moment was to allow the viewers a time for their own thoughts and feelings, when they did not need to be listening to the words of the songs, readings or introductions.

The 27th programme of this series, which was the 81st since *Stars* had started, turned out to be the last one because the following week's show was cancelled due to a blackout of the ITV screens. Appearing in a very different role from the one usually associated with him was comedian Dick Emery. He sang the classic Bing Crosby song 'The Bells of St Marys'. A fact not generally known about Dick Emery is that before the last war he trained as a singer for some time in Italy.

The date of show 81 was July 4 and *Stars* was going to be off the screens until September 19.

John Hanson

Anita Harris

Max Jaffa

Lovelace Watkins

Stuart Damon

Dick Emery

During the break two more enormous settings were created for *Stars On Sunday*. The first was the West Front of the building, in which the York Celebrations Choir performed, and the second was the pool and waterfall which was created for the dancer Patricia Ruanne. The West Front setting is the one that has been used possibly more times than any other single set. It consists of a two-storey building with six gigantic pillars, a domed roof to the house and a lake. The question has often been asked how such a big setting could be put into a television studio. The answer is a very simple but ingenious one and I do not intend to give the secret away.

The York Celebrations Choir had been founded in 1969 to take part in the celebrations being held in honour of the 1900th anniversary of the founding of the city of York. *Stars On Sunday* heard the choir and decided to record them for the programme. Two of Yorkshire's famous brass bands The Grimethorpe Colliery Brass Band and the Hammond Sauce Works Brass Band combined together with the 400 voices of the choir under the baton of Sir Vivian Dunn, a distinguished musician recognised as one of the leading brass band and choral conductors of our time. Also taking part in the visual recordings were the boy drummers and buglers of the third Huddersfield boys brigade. They were to be seen in such items as 'Battle Hymn of the Republic' and 'Onward Christian Soldiers'.

The other setting I mentioned was the pool and waterfall built for Patricia Ruanne to dance 'The Dying Swan'—tribute to Pavlova. To get this into the studio required a vast waterproof tank, which was the pool, and a large pump to recirculate the water from the pool back to the waterfall. It looked very effective on camera but proved to be too complicated a set-up to use very often and was discarded after relatively few sessions. For *Stars On Sunday* this is unusual because, being a middle-budgeted programme, settings take a great deal of the money and they therefore have to be utilised to the full.

Let us move on to the programme that opened the new series on September 19. The York Celebrations Choir closed the show with the 'Battle Hymn of the Republic', this was preceded by Patricia Ruanne's 'Dying Swan' and to mark the fact that it was Hospital Sunday Dame Anna Neagle read the Nurses' Prayer. Also in that edition were Bobby Bennett with the Young Ladies, Lovelace Watkins and Elizabeth Larner making her début.

The second edition of this series saw Dr Michael Ramsay, then Archbishop of Canterbury, taking part in the programme for the first time. Being the time of the Jewish New Year the London Jewish Male choir sang on the programme.

Stars on Sunday

During October two artistes from totally differing areas appeared on *Stars On Sunday*. From the Covent Garden opera house came the baritone singer Peter Glossop and from Scotland via *Dr Finlay's Casebook* came the actor Bill Simpson. November saw four new faces on the programme; the Australian singer Wilma Reading, quiz-master Hughie Green appearing as a singer and the three Beverley Sisters who had been persuaded to come together again for the *Stars On Sunday* viewers after virtually having retired from show business. The fourth new face was a unique feather in the cap for the programme when Admiral of the Fleet, The Earl Mountbatten of Burma consented to read 'For the Fallen' on the Remembrance Day edition. Used by way of introduction to the reading was the very emotive shot of the thousands of white crosses marking the graves of fallen British servicemen from Richard Attenborough's film *Oh what a lovely War!*

In November the Young Ladies of *Stars On Sunday* appeared dressed as nuns singing the song 'Whispering Hope'. The IBA felt it was not really appropriate for the singers to be dressed up as nuns and after one more programme the idea was dropped. What this event had done was to cause the Authority to look closely at *Stars On Sunday* and the criticism began to be levelled at it that the settings and costumes were too opulent and too theatrical for a religious programme. This debate was to continue in private for a few more weeks and then to culminate in a way that was to have a strange effect on the programme.

But we are beginning to run ahead of events so let us go back to December. This year *Stars* was to be transmitted over the Christmas period, so two Christmas orientated programmes were prepared. The first for Sunday December 19 and the second for Sunday December 26. The first one had Sir John Gielgud reading the Christmas Story and Harry Secombe, Stuart Gillies, Nina and Forbes Robinson singing songs that looked forward to Christmas, whilst the second programme was a spectacular carol concert.

A village setting had been built in the *Stars* studio and was covered with a special substance to give the effect of snow. Hanging above the studio were banks of rotating cylinders that disgorged finely chopped paper which, filtering through the lights, looked more like snow than snow itself. Strangely, although everyone was working under the hot studio lights the effect of all that white was enough to make one feel quite cold. It looked, on the control room monitors, extremely realistic and very pretty.

All worked quite well until one of the machines developed what can only be described as an asthmatic wheeze. It was a noise that cleared after a minute or two but for the first couple of minutes no sound could be used from the studio floor because of this appalling croaky wheeze. Eventually the only answer seemed to be to banish the said sick machine to a darker corner of the studio where it could not cause any more trouble. This operation was carried out successfully and the programme was eventually completed.

Taking part in this special edition were the Beverley Sisters and their three children; Shirley Bassey—singing a chorus of 'Oh Come All Ye Faithful'; the Poole Family; Hughie Green; Monica Rose; Bobby Bennett; The *Stars On Sunday* Singers; The York Celebrations Choir; The Salvation Army and two new stars Beryl Reid, who read from St Luke's Gospel, and Petula Clark. The final results were very well received by the viewers.

Three weeks on from that Christmas programme came *Stars On Sunday*'s 100th edition and the rather surprising climax to the debate that had been taking place about the settings and costumes. Somehow the press had got hold of the story and put out an account to the effect that the future of the programme was in doubt. *Stars On Sunday* seemed to be out of favour with everyone, excepting the viewing public for that 100th edition was watched by $18\frac{1}{2}$ million people and caused a unique event in the history of television. It put a religious programme into the top twenty along with such regulars as *Coronation Street*, *Crossroads*, and *This is Your Life*.

Three weeks later the same thing happened for watching the programme on the night of 6 February 1972 were over 20 million people. This is a figure that no religious programme has even come near, indeed *Stars On Sunday* never achieved it again. The office was flooded with letters asking that the programme should not be taken off. With the passing of the years one can look back to those days in early 1972 and realise that it would have been a very surprising move on the Authority's part to ban one of ITV's most successful programmes. But it is interesting to note how some of the programme's most ardent critics use its popularity with the viewers as a stick with which to beat it. *Stars* has never set out to be anything other than a programme to bring Christian comfort, warmth and joy to its viewers through the songs, Bible readings and introductory words that go to make up each edition. It does not exist to promote any one person's particular beliefs or desires.

The interest from the newspapers soon died down once it became apparent that the programme was not to be discontinued and the series carried on its run with the more usual average viewing figure of around 14 to 15 million. The last programme of this particular series was highlighted by having as the Bible reader the famous Canadian actor Raymond Burr. He was on one of his frequent trips to Europe and had come to Britain to help promote a newly designed wheelchair. His role in the detective series of *Ironside* had aroused in him a keen awareness of the problems facing people who have to spend their lives in a wheelchair, so when the Earl of Snowdon had asked for his co-operation in publicising this newly evolved aid for the chairbound he had willingly agreed. Raymond Burr and Gracie Fields brought the winter series of 1972 to a close. We were going off the air over the Easter period and would return on April 9 with a change in the transmission pattern.

Instead of being on for most of the year the programme was to work on a three months on air three months off air basis, which would help to relieve some of the pressures on the production team. When you realise that during the 135 weeks that had passed since the first edition had been transmitted on 17 August 1969, *Stars On Sunday* had been off the air for a total of only 21 weeks, you can begin to appreciate what those pressures were amounting to.

The Earl Mountbatten of Burma
Remembrance Day 1971

Rt Rev. The Lord Ramsay

Raymond Burr

The Beverley Sisters

Bill Simpson

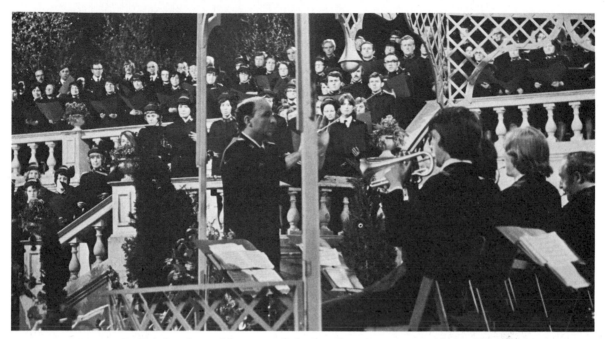

Major Leslie Condon with some of the band and songsters of the Salvation Army

Nina with her 8-year-old daughter Kirsa who appeared with her on Stars On Sunday in 1971, when she sang 'Away in a Manger'

The rate at which new star names to the programme were being introduced had by now begun to slow down. In the second programme on May 16 Frank Ifield made his first appearance for the viewers. Also Jean Grayston and Max Jaffa took part. Jean in private life is Mrs Max Jaffa. On this occasion they were not performing together, although in October 1972 Jean sang the lovely 'Panis Angelicus' whilst Max accompanied her on the violin. The week following saw the 120 members of the National Youth Brass Band of Great Britain taking part.

Another first appearance was made in the Whit Sunday edition of the programme by the singer/actress Georgia Brown. She sang 'My Mother's Sabbath Candles'. During the course of this song the special seven-branch Menorah is lit and to make sure that everything was done as it should be, *Stars On Sunday* had consulted the local Rabbi. It has always been considered of prime importance that any form of ritual used on the programme should be one hundred percent accurate.

In June the *Stars On Sunday* Great Choir was brought together with the Band of the Blues and Royals and the State Trumpeters. This was a gigantic operation to administrate and co-ordinate. There were close on 700 singers from a dozen or more different choirs who had to rehearse the various songs that were to be recorded. The location was Leeds Town Hall with its marble and gilt design and painted ceiling making an ideal setting for such a big choir. The band was to be under two different conductors. For the first day, when the State Trumpeters were there, it was their own conductor Major Jeans. The next day was under the baton of John Warburton from the York Celebrations Choir.

On the Saturday all the numbers involving the State Trumpeters were to be recorded as they could not be with us on the Sunday. A tall platform had been built out in the foyer of the hall so that a shot could be taken of three of the trumpeters with the domed and painted ceiling behind them. The moment arrived for the three lucky men to mount their precarious perch. Fortunately the camera was seeing them from the waist up only, because one of the trumpeters developed a dreadful shaking in his legs. Everyone thought he was going to fall off and just out of the camera's shot two hefty men were waiting to catch him if the worst did happen. Somehow he managed to get through it without disaster and when he shakily came down the ladder he admitted that he did not have a head for heights. I hope he has at some time had an opportunity to see one of those items because the end results were well worth all the discomfort he went through.

The next morning everybody was ready to start recording again at 10.00. We were scheduled to finish at 6.00 on Sunday evening and by 5.45 we had recorded every song except one which was 'Climb Every Mountain'. Should we leave that one? There was not time to rehearse it and then go for a recording. The cameramen, sound engineers and John Warburton and the director, Len Lurcuck, said 'Let's have a go.' So 'have a go' we all did. It was sung and played with such enthusiasm that the windows of the Town Hall were nearly blown out of their frames. I think that particular song is the only item on *Stars* ever to be done without some sort of rehearsal. The final notes died away at one minute to 6 and that was it. All over—until the next time. The series closed on the first Sunday in July with the Great Choir singing 'We're Marching to Zion'. *Stars* was to be off the air until September 10.

Frank Ifield

Georgia Brown

Stars on Sunday

The aims of *Stars On Sunday* had received endorsement from the leaders of the Anglican Church. This was shown by the willingness of both the Archbishop of Canterbury and the Archbishop of York to become regular readers in the series. It was now to be shown approval by the Roman Catholic church in the person of the late Cardinal John Heenan. Before deciding whether to take part in the programme Cardinal Heenan had insisted that he be allowed to watch some editions of *Stars*. He did this and then said 'This programme is worthwhile—a serious programme and very obviously a religious programme.'

The Cardinal arrived for his recording session not in the scarlet silk of a Cardinal but in the black cassock edged with red of a Bishop. He had selected the readings some time before and when the recording light went on he began to read from the Bible almost as if he were telling a story rather than giving a reading. It was extraordinary how still and quiet the studio had gone and how personal he managed to make those readings sound. If he had shown his approval of *Stars* by appearing in it, then the viewers showed their approval of his appearance by the number of letters that arrived in the office during the following week. Later in this same series Lord Soper made his début as a reader in the programme.

We had decided to prepare a special programme once again for Remembrance Sunday and a discussion had taken place in the production office as to who should be approached to read 'For the Fallen'.

Jess Yates suggested the Prime Minister, Edward Heath, should be asked, particularly bearing in mind his distinguished war record. Now it is a big enough problem obtaining the services of well-known actors and singers—their diaries are so heavily committed such a long way ahead—so how do you go about asking an even more heavily committed person such as the Prime Minister if he is both willing and has the time to record for *Stars On Sunday*? The answer is really quite simple—you write him a letter. This we did and it was my job to take it to 10 Downing Street and explain to the Prime Minister's Press Secretary what *Stars On Sunday* was all about.

On my arrival I was shown into a small sitting-room where soon I was joined by a secretary. The young lady asked me for the letter and enquired as to the purpose of the programme. I explained that each year *Stars On Sunday* presented a special Armistice Day edition to mark and remember the sacrifices that had been made by the armed forces and the civilian population during the two world wars. The centre piece to the programme was the reading of Laurence Binyon's poem 'For The Fallen'. It was our hope that, busy though he was, Edward Heath would be willing to read this poem for the programme. She agreed that Mr Heath was indeed extremely busy and asked if it was necessary for him to come to the Yorkshire studios in Leeds or if the reading could be filmed at number 10. I knew that the answer I had to give would be crucial to the final decision of whether he would or would not appear. *Stars* has never been recorded in any setting other than the home of *Stars On Sunday*, but the answer was really obvious the moment the question had been asked. If the Prime Minister is unable to record for us anywhere other than at number 10 then we will do it here.

For several weeks nothing was heard from Downing Street and then a letter arrived to say that Mr Heath would be pleased to take part in the programme and would I call at number 10 to finalise the details and, with his staff, select the room in which the filming would take place. The transmission date for the Remembrance programme was to be November 12 and the Downing Street letter had arrived at the end of October, which left very little time to organise things.

As soon as we entered it I knew that the Music Room was the room to use for the *Stars On Sunday* recording. The walls were covered in pale oyster fabric and there was a corner just to the right of the doors that had exactly the right look and 'feel' to it. A magnificent, highly polished grand piano stood near one of the windows and close to it was a music stand on which was displayed an original Mozart manuscript.

The recording date was fixed for Tuesday November 7 at 4.15 after the Prime Minister's question time in the House of Commons. We would be allowed to move our technical equipment in after lunch and set everything up.

The filming date arrived and Yorkshire's various production and management personnel, make-up and wardrobe staff descended on 10 Downing Street. What surprised me was that everybody and every piece of technical equipment had to go in through the front door. This was apparently for security reasons. By 3.30 everything was set up and ready to go.

The make-up lady had set out her box of tricks along the corridor in the butler's pantry and there was nothing else that could be done until the PM arrived. 4.15 came and went—no sign of Mr Heath. 4.30 came and went—still no Edward Heath. Just after 4.30 a message came through from the House of Commons to say that he had been delayed at question time but would be back at number 10 very soon.

A short while later he arrived at the front door. Introductions were made and we all moved into the music room. A poppy was placed in Mr Heath's button-hole and photographs were taken. He read through the poem a couple of times, for rehearsal and for the sound recordist to get a level on his voice, and then we were ready to set the cameras rolling. The cue was given and the Prime Minister began to read. In just under two minutes it was all over.

It was not until the film was in Leeds that we had the first opportunity of looking at it. Fortunately everything was well so it was edited into the programme the following night. On Sunday November 12 it was watched by $17\frac{1}{2}$ million viewers.

At about the same time we were setting up the Downing Street filming we had also reached agreement with the film star Deborah Kerr to take part in the programme as a Bible reader. The Sunday that she made her first appearance saw *Stars On Sunday* achieving the front cover of the *TV Times* with a picture of her.

On Sunday December 3 Janet Baker the world famous mezzo soprano made her début in *Stars*, whilst the following week saw the end of the series and the only appearance, to date, of David Frost who, like Vincent Price before him, read the 'Santa Claus letter'.

Cardinal John Heenan, late Archbishop of Westminster

Rt Hon. Edward Heath PC MBE MP
Remembrance Day 1972

Dame Janet Baker

David Frost

Band and State Trumpeters of the Blues and Royals.

Harry Secombe and 100 Boys Choir.

Pontefract Caledonian Pipe Band.

Her Serene Highness Princess Grace of Monaco reading nativity story.

The Children of Mary.

Lord Soper

Following on the change in the scheduling pattern for *Stars* the programme was off the screens all through the winter quarter and returned on April 8 with two newcomers, the American actor singer Stubby Kaye and the Rhosllanerchrugog Orpheus Male Voice Choir. Stubby appeared with the singers from the Leeds Thespians society and sang 'Sit down you're rockin' the boat'. The choir from Wales sang the beautiful 'Calon Lan'.

The setting used for them was the old abbey. It was built along one wall of the studio with black velvet curtains behind it, with a passageway running behind the curtain between it and the studio wall which led to the steep steps going up to the control room. Just before the choir were due to take up their position in the studio there was the sound of someone falling behind the curtain. We went round to see what had happened and found that one of the sound engineers was lying unconscious in the passageway. The duty nurse was sent for and she immediately called an ambulance which took him to hospital. Less than three weeks later we heard that he would not be coming back to work. He had died as a result of the stroke that had caused him to fall. He was just over forty.

The choir were unaware of the drama that had been taking place backstage and sang magnificently. For all of us working in the *Stars On Sunday* studio that night the singing of the Rhos Orpheus Choir has a very special meaning.

The programme suffered another loss when one of the young ladies of the backing singers was tragically killed in a car crash. Because of the ways *Stars* was made, with a number of different items being recorded in one session, we had a lot of songs that Penny Jewkes had taken part in with a number of different star soloists. The difficult decision had to be made, whether to scrap the items completely or ask Penny's parents if they would object to us using them. Jess Yates decided he would have to ask them for permission to transmit the songs. Their reply was most heart warming and moving, therefore the songs did appear in the series.

Easter Sunday fell late this year so *Stars* would be transmitting an Easter programme. The Archbishop of Canterbury read the story of Mary finding the empty tomb from St John's Gospel chapter 20 and the York Celebrations Choir sang the magnificent Easter Hymn from 'Cavaliera Rusticana'. Bev Jones, who had helped with the massed choirs, made his début as a professional singer on the programme.

In the same edition Hughie Green sang a number called 'The Wall of Old Joe Stone'. The moral to the song was basically on the theme of being a good neighbour. The writer had chosen to show this through a story line that concerned a dog and it had been decided that Hughie should sing the song with a dog on his lap. Now it so happened that at this time I owned a young sweet tempered but half-witted spaniel called Nimrod. I was asked to bring him to the studio for Hughie to sing with. I pointed out that he was not trained and might not be suitable. Apparently the fact that he looked right was more important than his training or lack of it—so he was cast for the part of friendly dog sitting on Mr Green's knee. I had given him a good brush and comb before taking him down in the car and had also reminded him about sitting and walking to heel—in fact all the things that a young well-trained dog should know. He had gone through his paces very well and had sat when told, looking at me with his big brown soulful eyes just as if he had won first prize in the obedience section of a dog show. So it was with a fair amount of confidence that I walked into the studio with Nimrod trotting just to the rear of my left heel. He and Hughie were introduced to each other and seemed to hit it off very well.

Having a lot of work to do in the office that day I left Nimrod with the floor manager and went to the office. About twenty minutes later the telephone rang and a distracted voice at the other end said 'Please will you come and do something about your dog.' I rushed down to the studio with dreadful pictures flashing through my mind of Nimrod having gone berserk and taken off Hughie's fingers, hand or even arm. I arrived somewhat breathless at the corner of the set, only to discover that the trouble was just the reverse. Nimrod really had taken to Hughie—so much so that every time Hughie started to sing Nimrod proceeded to try and give his face a good thorough wash. Under normal conditions this would have been a bit daunting for any singer but under the studio conditions it had become almost a fight for survival. As any of you that have dogs will know, when they get hot they pant and their tongues become so wet they almost run with perspiration. Under the studio lights Nimrod had become both very hot and rather restless. His black and white coat was shedding on to Hughie's once immaculate dark red velvet jacket and black trousers and what little make-up had been used was constantly being removed.

We had to make sure that Nimrod stayed put for the whole song. The answer was very simple and obvious—keep the lead on him and hide it in all that fluffy hair down the front of his chest. This was done and 'The Wall of Old Joe Stone' was recorded with Hughie and Nimrod both looking remarkably cool and composed.

Whilst writing about Nimrod it has reminded me of the experience

Bobby Bennett and Mark Curry had with a horse when recording for the programme a song called 'I've got my feet on God's Road'. The song was to be done as a duet and it had been decided that Bobby and Mark should sing it on horseback whilst moving slowly from one end of the paddock set to the other.

The red recording light went on and the cue to begin was given. During the musical introduction the horse, with its two passengers, should have slowly walked towards the camera. Absolutely nothing happened. It just stood there looking around and being so docile one might almost have thought it was asleep.

Some quick thinking had to be done. The camera script was rearranged so that the camera could move past the horse without showing its legs whilst Bobby and Mark bounced up and down as though the horse was walking. Once the final result was edited together it looked as though the horse had started at one end of the studio and slowly walked, with its two singing riders, to the other end.

That episode and the one with Nimrod emphasises the hazards of working with animals in television. This was brought home to us all again when we made 1973's Christmas show *The Glories of Christmas* but we will come to that in due course.

To leave animals and return to the humans in *Stars On Sunday*. This series was marked by the first appearance of the virtuoso violinist Yehudi Menuhin accompanied at the piano by his sister Hephzibah, and a few weeks later came the début of the New Zealand Opera star Kiri Te Kanawa, who has since then built herself an enormous world-wide following for her superb singing and interpretation of roles. Also in this series appeared Pearl Bailey, Rod McKuen, Roger Whittaker and that great lady of the British theatre Dame Edith Evans.

The wide span appeal of *Stars* is shown through the different people who appear on it. Dame Edith Evans one week, then Lord Soper, Julie Rogers, Gracie Fields, Kiri Te Kanawa and Lon Satton all taking part in the same edition.

Following Dame Edith's first appearance came that of Rod McKuen. His views concerning the importance of religion in a person's life seemed to stem from firmly held personal beliefs. At our first meeting I had brought with me one or two of his books and a list of the items that the viewers had requested he should sing. After going through that list and with further suggestions from him we arrived at a group of titles to be recorded for the series that fortunately included all the ones we had been asked for. It does not happen often, but just occasionally when you mention a particular song to a singer that has been specifically requested by the viewers they react by saying 'Oh no I can't sing that one now because my style has changed since I did it.' It seems that the bigger the artiste is as a star the less likely one is to get that sort of answer. Nearly always following Rod's appearances on *Stars* I get letters asking why he does not wear a dinner-jacket or a collar and tie and the answer is always the same, 'because that's me—it's not the clothes that make the man but what there is inside'.

The presentation of the programme had by now fallen into a well established pattern. There had been several co-presenters including Madeline Smith, Gabrielle Drake, Fiona Gaunt and on one edition Raymond Burr, and this series saw the first appearance of Ludmilla Nova who was to continue as co-presenter until the style of presentation change. The series closed on July 1 and was set for a twelve-week break.

Stubby Kaye with the Leeds Thespian Choir

Julie Rogers

Hughie Green with Nimrod

Roger Whittaker with one of the Stars singers

Rod McKuen

Bobby Bennett

The summer break passed with amazing speed and in what felt like no time at all *Stars* was back on the air. The new series was to be four weeks old before a different artiste for the viewers was to be introduced. This was the singer Brenda Arnau who sang the song from *Godspell* 'Day by Day'.

Starting in late September meant that we now had to be thinking very seriously about this year's Remembrance Day programme. By good fortune the crew of HMS Ark Royal were to be presented the freedom of the city of Leeds in a very short while, so I suggested that we made approaches to the Admiralty and to the Ship's Captain to see if they would be willing to record some items for *Stars*, in particular 'Eternal Father'.

Working with the Royal Navy turned out to be a most pleasant experience. They were so well organised and efficient. On the day fixed for the recording session coach loads of ratings, petty officers, officers and Royal Marines Bandsmen descended on the studios. There were close to 500 all told and the recording was carried out with military precision. The session was completed in the time allocated without any hitches and at the end they marched out to their buses and drove off to their next engagement.

I had told David Harries the Ark Royal's Anglican Chaplain that I was hopeful of obtaining the services of Sir Laurence Olivier as the reader for the Remembrance Day programme, because of his wartime connection with the Navy. David Harries suggested that I should enlist the help of the Captain of HMS Ark Royal and the Second Sea Lord at the Admiralty. I wrote to them explaining our intentions regarding the Remembrance Day programme and mentioning the hope we sustained that Lord Olivier would consent to take part. I do not know what they did or said but within a week Sir Laurence's personal assistant telephoned to ask if I could come to the offices of the National Theatre, with the reading, and to see if we could come to some arrangement for a recording date.

It was decided that I would call for him with a chauffered car at 12.15 and that he would be clear of the studios by 1.30. This allowed 25 minutes for a 15 minute journey, 20 for make-up and 30 minutes to rehearse and record a 2 minute reading.

The recording day arrived and at 11.45 I left the West End studios of ITN, which we had hired for the morning, and rode in the back of a large limousine to keep the appointment. At 12.15 precisely Sir Laurence appeared. I introduced myself and we both climbed into the back of the car. Just as we were about to move off Sir Laurence's PA rushed out carrying the great actor/manager's briefcase which he had left in his office. As soon as we were clear of the site and making our way to the Westminster Bridge area I realised that the journey was going to take every one of the 25 minutes that we had allowed. Every car, lorry and bus in London seemed to be converging on that particular route across the river. There was no alternative but to sit back, forget the valuable minutes ticking away and enjoy the opportunity of talking with a man who has become a theatrical legend in his own lifetime.

In what seemed no time at all we arrived at the studios. I glanced at my watch and saw to my horror that it was 1.5. The journey had taken over 45 minutes. We went into the building and Sir Laurence went straight to the make-up room. At 1.20 he was seated in the chair, poppy in lapel, reading through the poem as though there was all the time in the world available to us and not the 9 minutes recording time that was actually left. Having read it through a few times he glanced up and asked if we were ready to begin recording. The answer was a very definite yes. At 1.29 he had finished what is possibly the definitive interpretation of 'For the Fallen'. 'Do you want me to have another go at it?' he asked. I checked with the director who expressed complete satisfaction with the recording, so replied that we were most happy with the results. Sir Laurence made his way out of the studio thanking the technicians as he went.

He was just about to get into the waiting car when one of ITN's security staff arrived at the door with his briefcase, which had been left in the make-up room. He took the case and climbed into the car. As I was waiting for it to draw away I saw the briefcase being opened and extracted from it a small package of what looked like sandwiches and an apple.

The combination of Olivier, Janet Baker singing 'Abide With Me', the crew of HMS Ark Royal and the opening prayer from the Archbishop of Canterbury made 1973's Remembrance Day programme an especially memorable one.

By this stage of the series we were beginning to put together the final details for the Christmas programme *The Glories of Christmas*. Jess Yates had been to Monaco to be presented to Princess Grace and to ask if she would be willing to take part in this programme and at the same time record some Bible readings for inclusion in *Stars On Sunday*. He had returned with the news that the Princess would read the Nativity story for *The Glories of Christmas* and, if time permitted, would also read for *Stars*. The readings Her Highness selected were 'The Prayer of St Francis of Assisi', the 'Parable of the labourers in the Vineyard' which is apparently one of her favourite passages from the Gospels and from St Matthew chapter 5, part of the 'Sermon on the Mount', the Beatitudes.

The date agreed upon with the Palace in Monaco for Princess Grace's readings was the Monday morning in the week of Princess Anne's and Captain Mark Phillips' wedding. Prince Rainier and Princess Grace were to be in London as guests at the wedding and she had agreed to set aside the Monday morning for *Stars On Sunday*.

I was associate producer for the show and had special responsibility for the setting up of the Princess Grace studio in London and, once again, the animals that were to be used in the Nativity. Reading the list of animals needed for that sequence you would have thought the *Stars On Sunday* production office was going into business as a cross between a farm and a zoo. A brief rundown showed it as follows. Dogs, camels, chickens, cockerels, donkey, doves, cows, sheep, horses and lambs. The only difficult ones to track down were the lambs and the camels. It seems that early November is not the best time of the year to be looking for new-born lambs. We were successful however and found a farmer not too far away whose sheep had lambed very recently. The camels were the biggest problem because they apparently can be very evil-tempered beasts and to have some wandering round a studio all day could prove quite hazardous to the humans they came in contact with. I was beginning to despair of finding a sweet-tempered camel that could be safely used on a studio set when a source I had already spoken to contacted me again to say that they had a young one which would probably be safe enough but its keeper would have to be with it all the time.

The Saturday morning of recording arrived and by 9.30 various horse boxes, cattle trucks and a camel transporter had turned up at the scene dock entrance to studio 4. The sheep were turned out on to the clad rostrum hillside where Howard Dawson, the designer, had thoughtfully placed clumps of real grass and they passed the day quietly munching through it and, so we discovered afterwards, some plastic grass matting that was also covering the hillside. The cows stood in the byre that had been built for the stable sequence, whilst all around were placed very well schooled doves and surprisingly placid chickens and cockerels. The dogs were kept back until just before the actual recording time.

The first tableau to be recorded was of Mary and Joseph looking for a place for the night where The Baby could be born. This went through quite well without any difficulty from either humans or donkey. Next came the shepherds on the hillside seeing the star over the stable— again no problem. Then came the wise men riding from the East. A complication became immediately apparent when one of the wise men, or kings, attempted to mount his horse. There was a lot of noise and clatter from that corner of the studio and we discovered that disconcertingly enough one of the horses had never been ridden before and was certainly not prepared to let this Saturday be the first occasion in its life when it would submit to the weight of a human being on its back. There was no option but to let one of the kings walk on his journey to Bethlehem. The camel, with keeper in attendance suitably attired in a striped hooded cloak, behaved as though it had spent its entire life working in a television studio. The final outcome of that day's recording was twelve minutes of beautiful pictures which depicted very well the humble simplicity of the first Christmas day.

On the Sunday the Huddersfield Choral Society came to the studios to record their contribution to the *Glories of Christmas* and some choir items for *Stars On Sunday*. A scene crew and myself made off to London to set up the studio for the following morning.

Her Highness's dark blue limousine Rolls-Royce arrived at the front door of ITN promptly and from it emerged Princess Grace. Behind her came the Principality's Consul General, her lady in waiting, her hairdresser and his assistant. The Princess and the two hairdressers went off to the dressing-room to complete her preparations for the recording. When she walked on to the studio floor some forty minutes later the effect was quite remarkable. The dress was a stunning creation in red, green and gold. The atmosphere in the studio had changed as dramatically as does a garden between winter and summer.

Everyone seemed to be aware that what was taking place was a piece of television history. Since her retirement from Hollywood at the time of her marriage to Prince Rainier she had always declined all offers to appear in films or television programmes other than some documentary pieces that were made to help causes close to her heart. Yet here she was on a television set about to read for both the viewers of the *Glories of Christmas* and *Stars On Sunday*. When the Nativity reading had been completed she retired to her dressing-room to change into a simple black dress and then she was back on the set ready for the *Stars On Sunday* readings.

These, like the reading of the Nativity, went through faultlessly. Within ten minutes of them being completed she and her entourage were on their way.

Sir Laurence Olivier

The Choir and band of HMS Ark Royal. In the foreground is the
Reverend David A. Harries RN. Remembrance Day 1973

State Trumpeters and the Band of the Blues and Royals. Remembrance
Day 1973

Stars on Sunday

The spring series opened on April 21 with the programme in which Princess Grace made her début for the *Stars On Sunday* audience. This edition opened with the lovely hymn 'Non Nobis Domine' sung by the 200-strong boys' choir of the Pueri Cantores. They were stood on the ballroom staircase filling the screen with the vibrant colour of their scarlet cassocks and their well scrubbed shining faces. Following on from their hymn was the ever popular 'The Lord is my Shepherd', sung by Janet Baker. Then came Yehudi Menuhin, followed by Lon Satton singing of old-time religion with the aid of *Stars On Sunday* singers.

The SOS singers, as they were referred to in the programme's production office, had been under the capable musical direction of Nigel Brooks for the past two years. There are always nine of them and, with very few exceptions, almost every edition of *Stars* sees them as backing singers for one or two of the soloists.

Her Highness was followed by Vince Hill's rendering of 'One Hand One Heart' and that evening's edition closed with the Royal Navy Choir of HMS Ark Royal singing 'Oh God Our Help In Ages Past'.

Another massed choir operation, scheduled to be recorded during the last weekend in June, was now beginning to get underway. The thinking behind it was that the choir should be made up from the many varied organisations that help to form the community. Approaches had been made to: The British Legion, The Fire Service, The Police, The Nursing Organisations, The WRVS, The Scouts, Guides, Boys' Brigade, Air Force, Army and Navy, The Salvation Army, The National Association of Lifeboats and the Miners—who have some splendid voiced choirs. The Leeds Choral Society, The York Celebrations Choir and The Doncaster Wheatsheaf girls' choir were to provide the nucleus of the choral singing. Donald Hunt was asked to be the musical director and conductor for this occasion whilst the band was to be provided by the Salvation Army from Sheffield Citadel division under their bandmaster Brian Towse.

The weekend for the recording arrived and Leeds Town Hall had again been adapted to work as a television studio. The choirs and band had arrived and the complicated, but necessary, business of sorting everyone out in their differing heights had begun. The sizing and voicing operation having been finished and everybody correctly positioned, the recording got underway.

Surprisingly enough the two days' work was completed without any mishaps and by fifteen minutes before the end of the scheduled time allowed, every item was satisfactorily recorded. None of the hymns recorded over that weekend was to appear on screen until the autumn series of *Stars* had begun.

To return to the current summer series. The third edition saw the first appearance of Valerie Masterson, from Sadler's Wells Opera, and Robert Lloyd from Covent Garden. The following week the Chinese opera singer Soo Bee Lee, who had settled in England, made her début. From Manchester, for the programme on June 2, had come the Junior Salvation band and choir none of whom was older than twelve. Appearing in that same edition with them was Princess Grace reading the 'Prayer of St Francis of Assisi'. Sunday June 9 Les Dawson appeared with a small group of children and sang to them the song 'The Architect'.

Jess Yates' time with the programme was coming to an end and he had asked Moira Lister to introduce the edition for June 30, which was the second evening of the massed choir recordings at the town hall. Anthony Valentine had been asked to present the final edition of the summer series. He was surprised, after his wealth of experience as an actor, to discover how different it was facing the cameras as oneself and reading out the viewers' requests for the various hymns and readings. He did it with his usual professional expertise and the office received many letters saying how much people had enjoyed seeing him introduce the programme.

The next series was not scheduled for transmission until November 17 so the production office were able to take a good break for holidays.

During the summer break Robert Dougall, who had recently retired from the BBC agreed, despite his heavy commitments, to become the new presenter of the programme. In addition to a new presenter the programme also required an accompanist, to play the organ. I asked Bob Hartley, who had often played for *Junior Showtime*, if he would take on this job and also become one of the music advisers to *Stars On Sunday*. The answer was yes. Nigel Brooks agreed to continue as the other music adviser with particular reference to the backing singers. Monsignor Michael Buckley and Reverend Brandon Jackson were happy to continue as the programme's religious advisers, so we had a complete team ready to start putting together material for the new series.

In the meantime Brandon Jackson had been busy. He had approached Dr Donald Coggan, who was shortly to move from the Archbishopric of York to that of Canterbury, to ask if he would consider taking part in the series as a speaker rather than a reader. His Grace had liked the idea. The proposal was that he should appear in 12 of the programmes out of the 13, taking as an overall theme the Ten Commandments and their value to us in our lives today in the 20th century. Somebody asked how the Ten Commandments could be spread over 12 programmes. The answer was really very simple. Programme 1 would be a general introduction to the subject; one programme for each of the Commandments and one in which His Grace would be talking to the American astronaut James Irwin, who was visiting Britain for a short while.

I knew that since his experience in outer space James Irwin had become such a convinced believer in God and Christianity that he had helped to set up and run an evangelical organisation in the States called High Flight. I felt that a meeting between him and the Archbishop on *Stars On Sunday* was well worth watching and listening to. It would be a complete departure from the format that had become so established during the past five years, but then so were the Archbishop's talks. The letters received in the office during the course of this series indicated that my feeling had been right.

The first recording day in London, for this new series, was to be followed by a two-day session in Leeds so there was a lot of toing and froing between both towns. The rehearsals for the Nigel Brooks singers were taking place in a London rehearsal studio at the same time as we were setting up the recording studio for Kenneth More and Joseph Cotten. Kenneth More was to record before lunch and Joseph Cotten immediately after lunch. Both sets of recordings were completed without any mishaps and then it was back to the rehearsal studio to see how things were getting on there.

The solo artistes who were being backed by the singers were John Lawrenson and Kamahl. John was a well-known name and voice from the world of radio and the concert platform but had never been on *Stars On Sunday* before. His voice was particularly suited to the works of Sir Arthur Sullivan, such as 'The Lost Chord', so this was to be included among the items he was doing for us. Kamahl, who was a very big star name in Australia, was to open the first edition of the autumn series with the song 'One Hundred Children'. In the same programme there was another singer from Australia, James Pegler who, with the Nigel Brooks singers, sang the popular tune 'Put your hand in the hand of the Man from Galilee'.

By the end of Friday 8 November every item that was needed for the programme on the 17th was ready apart from Harry Secombe's song, which was to be done on the Monday. Robert Dougall was due in Leeds to link the items together and read the requests and dedications on Tuesday 12th and after that the programme would be complete. So after a busy and hectic week we went to our homes on Friday for a quiet weekend. On Sunday my telephone rang and at the other end was Harry Secombe's agent. He had rung to tell me that Harry had very bad tracheitis and was unable to sing a note so would not be able to record for the programme next morning. The doctors had told him to have a complete rest for at least two weeks and that under no circumstances was he to try and do any singing. My heart sank into my boots. Because of the Archbishop's theme in his first talk I needed the song 'No Man Is an Island'. I thanked him for ringing me and sent my best wishes to Harry for a speedy recovery and then sat down to think. Who, at less than twenty-four hours notice, would be able to come up to Leeds and sing that particular song?

My thoughts went at once to John Lawrenson who, like Harry, had an operatic voice and who, I hoped, just might know the song. The answer was 'Yes' he would come and 'No' he didn't know the song but would learn it if I could arrange for a copy to be left for him at the Leeds hotel, which he expected to reach during the early hours of the Monday morning. I put the telephone down with a sigh of relief and then drove to the studios to pick up a copy of 'No Man Is an Island' to take round to the hotel.

On Monday morning at 9.00 I met John in the canteen at the studios and asked if he was happy to go into the studio at 10 o'clock and do the recording. He said that he was and that he thought he would remember the words. The only thing was that as he had learnt them under the shower in his hotel bathroom he might need to hear the sound of running water to refresh his memory.

At 10.00 am John went on to the set and proceeded to give a faultless rendering of a far from easy song. Sitting in the control room it was impossible to believe that less than seven hours earlier he had never seen one note or word of it before. It just goes to show what a really professional artiste can manage. I shall always remember his help on that occasion with gratitude. Incidentally Harry Secombe was able to join us on the series by the sixth edition which was transmitted on December 29.

On the Tuesday Bob Dougall took up for the first time his role as presenter of *Stars On Sunday*. It was, as he put it, a refreshing change to be dispensing 'good news' as opposed to the 'doom and gloom' he had so recently been presenting as the BBC's senior news reader. He had taken a great deal of trouble over the preparation of his script and when the cue to begin was given sailed through it as though he had been introducing *Stars On Sunday* for years. The edition transmitted on November 17 was watched by close on 14 million people and the series continued to maintain around that number of viewers during its run of 13 weeks.

Besides persuading stars, who had not been on *Stars On Sunday* before, to appear on the programme, we were welcoming back firm favourites such as Moira Anderson, Rolf Harris, Kenneth McKellar and Anita Harris. Also returning after a long absence was the Irish soprano Patricia Cahill and the distinguished actor Sir John Gielgud. Among the new faces to the programme were Dame Flora Robson, Douglas Fairbanks junior, Edward Woodward and Frank Finlay.

My first meeting with each of these three actors took place in their respective theatres. Mr Fairbanks liked the idea of the programme and so we proceeded to the selection of the readings. It was at this point that I discovered that along with all his other numerous activities, for he has many business as well as theatre and film interests, he had found time to become a student of the Bible. Discussing the merits and de-merits of particular texts from the Bible I felt as though I were talking with a theologian rather than an actor. Apparently his extensive knowledge of the Book came from his childhood days when he had been sent to both the Catholic and Protestant Sunday schools—why both I did not discover. The parables of Jesus seemed very much to Mr Fairbanks' liking particularly the parable of the sower from St Matthew's Gospel.

My next meeting backstage of a theatre was very different. I had gone to the Queen's in Shaftesbury Avenue to see Frank Finlay in *Saturday, Sunday Monday*. When I went round to the stage door afterwards it was in the company of many admiring fans who were waiting for autographs. I was shown into Frank Finlay's dressing-room and held my discussion with him whilst he was removing his make-up and changing back from the Italian he had been for the past two-and-a-half hours on stage.

Our discussion was interrupted by the stage door keeper who wanted to lock up the theatre for the night so we decided to continue our talk in the lounge at my hotel. When we arrived we went through to the bar and ordered a pot of tea and then got down to the business of deciding which of the suggested readings I had brought with me should be done for the programme. Frank was particularly keen on the account in St Luke's Gospel of the first occasion of the Lord's Prayer. As in most hotels up in my room was a Bible, placed there by the Gideons, so I went up to get it. On my return we sorted through the Gospels until we found the appropriate text. Sometimes Frank would read out a few verses and sometimes I would until we eventually settled on some readings that suited both of us.

It was by now about 1.00 am so he drove off to his home and I went up to my room. It was only then that I realised how strange our discussion must have seemed to the other occupants of the lounge bar. Two gentlemen sat in a corner with a pot of tea at midnight quoting bits of the Bible at each other. I wonder what they made of it all?

Mind you, I think the international telephone operator between Leeds and Sierra Leone probably overhead the strangest conversation, between myself and Vince Hill. On his return from there he was coming straight to Leeds to appear in *Stars* and it proved necessary that to make certain about one of his songs I should talk with him before he made the trip. It was to do with the lyrics of the song and Vince was singing them to me down the telephone. Now on that particular route there is a two to three second delay between the time the speaker utters his words and the listener hears them. It's just about understandable if you talk in short sharp sentences and then wait a moment or two before starting again but when it's singing, where the note is sustained, it all runs into itself. As a result of the total confusion that ensued that particular song never did see the light of day on the programme.

Another theatre visit was made to see Edward Woodward who was coming to the *Stars* studio to sing rather than read for the programme. The theatre was the Piccadilly where a few weeks earlier the musical *Gypsy* had been playing. The 'star' dressing-room had been occupied by Angela Lansbury and it had been decorated to her taste. When I walked into it to meet Edward Woodward who, I must admit, I still at that time identified very much with the tough character of Callan he had been playing for so long on television I was rather taken aback by all the pretty chintzes and delicate floral wallpaper. It was he who told me that the decor was Miss Lansbury's choice. He had very definite ideas on the items he wished to sing for the programme. With the exception of 'Morning has Broken' they were all hymns and were ones which he knew well from his days of singing in a church choir. On the agreed date for the recordings he, like Harry Secombe, was unable to perform because of a throat infection so the session had to be postponed until later. It was not until February 2 that Edward Woodward made his début for the *Stars On Sunday* audience with the hymn 'The King of Love my Shepherd is'.

On the choral side of the programme the Leeds Parish Church choir had recorded for the show and down from Scotland had come the world famous Glasgow Phoenix choir. Amongst the selection they offered for the programme was the lovely 'All on an April evening'. During the course of this winter series Nigel Brooks made his *Stars* début as a soloist fronting his own singers, with the song 'I thank the Lord for everything'.

The Bachelors

Les Dawson

Anthony Valentine
Bible Reader and Presenter 1974

Robert Dougall

Astronaut James Irwin reading Psalm 121

Kenneth More

Joseph Cotten

Kamahl

Anthony Quayle

Kenneth McKellar

Douglas Fairbanks

Dame Flora Robson

Edward Woodward

Christopher Lee

Rostal and Schaeffer

Stars on Sunday

The series ended on February 16 but as the next one was scheduled to start on April 6 there was not any time to sit back and rest. Bob Dougall had agreed to continue introducing the programme for this next series but was finding his time increasingly taken up with his work for the Royal Society for the Protection of Birds and his writing commitments. The Archbishop's talks had been very successful and, after discussion with the religious advisors, it was decided to continue the idea of a short talk but to share it between representatives of the three major denominations. The Church of England was represented by the Bishop of Coventry Dr Cuthbert Bardsley; the Catholic church by Bishop Christopher Butler OSB and the Methodist church by Lord Soper.

The first edition of the new series re-introduced Howard Keel and Kenneth McKellar to the *Stars* audience. The four titles we settled on with Howard Keel were the Welsh hymn 'All through the night', the spiritual 'Were you there', 'The 23rd Psalm' arranged by Malotte, and the moving song 'Goin Home' set to the music of Dvorak's 'New World Symphony'. This particular one had a special significance for Howard Keel, because not very long before his trip to Britain he had been asked to sing it for the funeral of a very close relative. The setting that had been decided on was the *Stars On Sunday* library, which has a large pair of double doors leading into it from a rotunda or circular hallway. The idea was for Mr Keel to walk through from the rotunda into the library and then to start singing. This we had to alter somewhat because he was so tall that when he came through the doorway he had to duck his head, so he started his move just inside the library doors. This same edition saw the début of the children's choir of St Richard's with St Andrew's Church of England school from Ham near Richmond, Surrey.

Two questions that are frequently asked about the programme are, who are the most popular artistes and which are the most requested songs. The first question does not get answered but the songs are included in this book.

The edition transmitted on April 20 marked the début of Christopher Lee on the programme in a rather unusual role for this actor who is probably best known for his portrayal of the sinister and macabre. I had made my initial approaches to him with a view to his being one of this series' Bible readers. I was surprised to find that he has a great knowledge and love of music and a very good baritone voice. He was happy to read for the programme but said that he would also like to sing on it, so we set about sorting out suitable numbers. The three we agreed on were 'Jerusalem', 'A Mighty fortress is our God' and the old spiritual 'I've got a Robe'. This selection was arrived at by the simple process of elimination. I sat in a large wing chair in Mr Lee's drawing room whilst he sang snatches of numerous different songs, hymns, oratorios, operas and spirituals. It was a virtuoso one-man concert that lasted almost an hour and displayed not only his versatility but his extensive knowledge of European languages. In fact the hymn he sang for the viewers on April 20 was in its original German, as written by Martin Luther.

The Beverley Sisters returned to *Stars On Sunday* to appear in this series and have since continued as regular guests. It is always a pleasure to work with them as their whole approach to the programme is so well considered and professional. We have a meeting before their visits to the Leeds studios and on every occasion when we have got together to decide on the contents for their recording session they have already worked out suggestions for my approval. So I sit and listen to their skilled harmony singing and find it very difficult to pick one particular song in preference to another. Fortunately I have the viewers' requests and each programme's theme to help me make a choice. I have met the Bevs many times and have never seen them dressed other than in matching clothes which, of course, has made me wonder how they manage it. Apparently over the years they have built up an enormous wardrobe of clothes, even down to matching dressing-gowns, and these are used for their professional and public appearances. You will never see them, even just two of them, dressed other than identically.

In addition to the Bevs returning to *Stars*, the ladies were represented in the series by Moira Anderson, Anita Harris, Dame Flora Robson and four newcomers to the programme. From the cabaret and light entertainment world Salena Jones and Diana Kirkwood whilst from radio and the concert platform came Valerie Monese and Rita Morris. Rostal and Schaefer and the Jacques Loussier trio provided the instrumental items and John Lawrenson, John Boulter, Nigel Brooks, Stuart Gillies and Harry Secombe were the solo artistes for whom the Nigel Brooks singers provided choral backing. Rod McKuen during the course of his 1975 tour of Britain came to the Leeds Grand Theatre and took time out to visit *Stars On Sunday* to record some more of his own special brand of songs for the programme.

Anthony Quayle joined the distinguished list of actors who had appeared as Bible readers for the programme. The feature film Moses, in which Anthony Quayle was portraying Moses's brother Aaron, had recently been shooting in Israel and, from the tone of his conversation, he had been deeply impressed by the atmosphere of the Holy Land. To visit the places which are written about in the Bible and to see the same scenery that Christ and his disciples saw somehow helps to make the

Gospels seem more immediate and relevant to today—was how he put it. One of the things I have become aware of, while producing *Stars On Sunday*, is how thoroughly the actors and acresses asked to appear as Bible readers study the particular excerpts they are going to read and what an extensive knowledge of the Bible many of them possess. Mr Quayle proved to be no exception to this.

The spring series was due to end on the first Sunday in July but because the programme scheduled for May 25 was lost, due to an industrial dispute, the series did not end until July 13. With the close of the last edition Robert Dougall was able to take a well-earned break. His support and co-operation had been of invaluable help.

In exactly nine Sundays' time the programme would be back on air for its next three months' run, which would end just before Christmas. It was decided to ask Wilfred and Mabel Pickles to present the bulk of this series, which was going to have guest presenters for three of the programmes. The idea of introducing the programme appealed to them both for they had been regular viewers of *Stars On Sunday* for a long time and had a high regard for it. I had asked Miss Gracie Fields if she would be willing to record the opening music for the winter programmes and she had agreed to fly over from Capri especially for the session.

I have mentioned, earlier in this book, how long it can sometimes take between the first approaches being made to an artiste and their appearing on the programme. The first programme of the winter series on September 14 saw the début of Bing Crosby in *Stars On Sunday*. In early August I had heard that Bing Crosby was over here to make a record. I contacted his record producer and it was left that if Mr Crosby was willing and able to appear on the programme he would give me a ring at the Leeds office.

A few days later I was sitting in the canteen at Leeds when one of the secretaries from the office came in looking slightly flushed and walked across to where I was sitting. 'I'm sorry to disturb you,' she said, 'but I've got a fellow on the telephone who won't leave a message and insists on talking to you personally.' 'Who is it?' I asked. She gave a little disbelieving laugh. 'Well he says he's Bing Crosby,' she replied. With that I leaped to my feet and broke the world record for the 100 yard sprint back to my office. I regained my breath picked up the phone and said in as calm a voice as I could manage. 'Good afternoon Mr Crosby can I do anything for you?' The reply was brief but very pleasant to hear 'Yes, when can we get together and sort out something for this programme of yours?' And that was it.

The recording session was being done in Studio 2 and from the moment he came on to the set it was packed with studio personnel who had all found a legitimate excuse for being there. We went through the songs and readings without any problems and finished the session close on 12. We went for a pre-lunch drink in the club bar. While we were there I mentioned that he had many fans amongst the members of the canteen staff and that they would love to see him for a few moments. 'Well let's go and see them,' he said. So off we went into the canteen where he shook hands and spoke with everyone who came up to him. He went along the serving counter meeting all the staff from the manager and head chef down to the most junior washer-up and signed many autographs.

The edition on September 14 saw the return to *Stars* of Roger Whittaker and Dame Anna Neagle as a reader, although later on in the series she was to introduce the programme as a guest presenter for a special ladies' edition marking the fact that 1975 was International Women's Year. The other two guest presenters were to be Gordon Jackson, for St Andrew's day, and Kenneth More for Remembrance Sunday. Both of them also appeared as readers as did fellow Scot, Andrew Cruickshank. Other readers in this series were Raymond Burr, returning after an absence of some three years, Princess Grace of Monaco, Miss Evelyn Laye, Trevor Howard and James Stewart.

Mr Stewart's appearance caused an enormous flood of mail into the *Stars* office. He had read a piece on the programme called 'The Lord ruleth Me'. It had, he said, a very special meaning for him and had brought both he and his family great strength and comfort at a time of terrible tragedy when their son had been killed in the war in Vietnam. When we were in the studio for the recording with Mr Stewart I asked him if he would introduce the reading himself. He asked me what he should say and I suggested that he should tell the viewers exactly how the reading had come into his possession and what it meant to him. He did just that and with such sincerity and sensitivity that within a matter of a few days the office was flooded with requests for copies to help strengthen people who had suffered the loss through death of someone they had loved dearly. On the Monday morning after the programme had been transmitted we were dictating the reading down the phone on several occasions to people who required it more quickly than the postman could bring it to them. By the end of the week some three thousand copies had been sent off.

On the singing side of the programme the great Spanish soprano Victoria de Los Angeles made her début in this series as did the popular Irish songstress Dana. Also from Ireland came the beautiful singing of

Stars on Sunday

Bernadette Greevy whilst from America came the magnificent baritone voice of Sherrill Milnes. In addition to American opera being represented, the American theatre and cabaret scene were strongly shown in the persons of Val Pringle and Eartha Kitt. Val was currently starring in the London West End musical based on Gilbert and Sullivan's famous light opera The Mikado.

Eartha Kitt, on the occasion of her recording, was the complete professional that one has come to expect over the years. Her style is disarmingly relaxed and easy but it takes a great deal of practice and rehearsal to achieve it. I had had a couple of meetings with her at her hotel to finalise the items which she was going to sing.

Among the most popular items in the programme were the paddock old-pioneering songs and during the series these were presented by Bobby Bennett and Barry Kent, who were making a welcome return to *Stars*. Another popular singer who returned during the winter months was Frank Ifield. Frank brought his own special brand of brightness to his interpretation of the numbers and also managed to surprise me by suggesting some old song titles that I had never heard of. During the years we have transmitted well over a thousand different songs, all of them with some bearing on the programme's different themes, and it was pleasant to discover that the supply had not yet run out.

The Christmas programme was marked by the first appearance of Virginia McKenna. She, in company with some young children from Miss Jean Pearce's school, sang the simple little carol 'Away in a Manger'. Princess Grace, Bing Crosby, Harry Secombe, Kenneth McKellar and, another newcomer to the programme, Ethna Campbell brought the series to a close.

As usual I had been studying the feelings of the viewers, through their letters, and one thing was very apparent—their liking for the introduction of guest presenters on the programme. I therefore decided to enlarge on this during the run of the spring series, which was scheduled to begin on 4 April 1976, and asked Gordon Jackson, Moira Anderson, Robert Dougall and Wilfred Pickles if they would present this series to the viewers on an alternating basis. Because it meant less time involvement, Bob Dougall was able to accept and I was very pleased to welcome him back to introduce the guests for the programme on May 2.

Gordon Jackson opened the series and in that first edition introduced three new stars to the audience. They were Glynis Johns, Louis Jourdan and Val Doonican. Miss Johns asked if in addition to the Bible extracts she could read 'Desiderata', because it was a piece that she found gave her great comfort and she felt that it may do the same for the viewers.

It was approaching two years since Joseph Cotten had first read it on the programme and there had been many requests for it to be read again, so I was happy to agree to her request. Louis Jourdan proved to be extremely knowledgeable about the Bible and had a strong preference for the book of Ecclesiastes.

Val Doonican brought to the programme his warmth and a delightful selection of songs, most of which related to children, for he is very much a family man and his choice of songs reflected this.

The first half of the series saw the débuts of Brian Rix, Ricki Lee, George Hamilton IV, Slim Whitman and Frankie Vaughan. Bob Monkhouse, after a long absence, returned and confirmed his versatility as a performer by both singing and reading for the viewers. Slim Whitman and George Hamilton IV visited the *Stars* studio during the course of their extensive British tours and introduced into the programme a distinctive brand of country music with songs that have a simple directness of approach in their lyrics. Such as 'The Family Bible' and 'Carried on the Shoulders of the Shepherd'. Frankie Vaughan chose for his first appearance the lovely ballad 'Sunrise Sunset' and especially asked for his song 'When I look into your Eyes' to be dedicated to those whose anniversaries it was on June 6 for that day he too celebrated his silver wedding anniversary. If there are any of you who saw that programme and wondered who the baby in the photograph was—well that was Frankie's own granddaughter.

In the seven years since *Stars On Sunday* made its first appearance on television it has been seen by a total of some 3,500 million people, has presented close on 5,000 singers and readers, over 250 different soloists, and has taken 2,000 hours of making time to present almost 6,000 minutes of on air time. But it is not, for all this, a programme that concerns itself with statistics but with people. It is made for the viewer from Grimsby who asks for Harry Secombe to sing 'Bless This House', for the one in Blackpool who asks for Gracie Fields to sing something especially for her grandparents' diamond wedding or for the man in Aberdeen or the woman in Cornwall who want to hear Sir John Gielgud read from Christ's Sermon on the Mount. *Stars On Sunday* is enjoyed by millions but is made each week for the pleasure and comfort of each individual viewer who may be watching it by their fireside at home.

Bing Crosby

Bernadette Greevy

Andrew Cruickshank

Victoria de los Angeles

Trevor Howard

Bob Monkhouse

Brian Rix

Virginia McKenna and the children who sang 'Away in a Manger' with her. Christmas 1975

Frankie Vaughan

Wilfred and Mabel Pickles

Dame Anna Neagle presenting the programme

James Stewart reading 'The Lord Ruleth Me'

Val Doonican

Gordon Jackson presenting the programme

The most requested Hymns are:

The Old Rugged Cross
Abide with me
Ave Maria
Amazing Grace
The Twenty-Third Psalm
Jerusalem

The Old Rugged Cross

On a hill far away stood an old rugged cross,
The emblem of suffering and shame.
And I love that old cross, where the dearest and best,
For a world of lost sinners was slain.

So I'll cherish the cross, the old rugged cross,
Till my trophies at last I lay down,
I will cling to the cross, the old rugged cross,
And exchange it some day for a crown.

Oh that old rugged cross, so despised by the world,
Has a wonderous attraction for me,
For the dear lamb of God left His glory above,
To bear it to dark Calvary.

So I'll cherish the old rugged cross,
Till my trophies at last I lay down,
I will cling to the old rugged cross,
And exchange it some day for a crown.

In that old rugged cross stained with blood so divine,
A wonderous beauty I see.
For 'twas on that old rugged cross Jesus suffered and died,
To pardon and sanctify me.

So I'll cherish the cross, the old rugged cross,
Till my trophies at last I lay down,
I will cling to to cross, the old rugged cross,
And exchange it some day for a crown.

To the old rugged cross, I will ever be true,
And it's shame and reproach gladly bear,
Then He'll call me some day, to my home far away,
Where His glory for ever I'll share.

Abide with me

Abide with me; fast falls the eventide,
The darkness deepens; Lord, with me abide;
When other helpers fail, and comforts flee,
Help of the helpless, O abide with me.

Swift to its close ebbs out life's little day;
Earth's joys grow dim, its glories pass away;
Change and decay in all around I see;
O thou who changest not, abide with me.

I need Thy presence every passing hour;
What but Thy grace can foil the tempter's power?
Who like Thyself my guide and stay can be?
Through cloud and sunshine, Lord, abide with me.

I fear no foe with Thee at hand to bless;
Ills have no weight, and tears no bitterness;
Where is death's sting? Where, grave, thy victory?
I triumph still, if Thou abide with me.

Hold Thou Thy Cross before my closing eyes;
Shine through the gloom, and point me to the skies;
Heaven's morning breaks, and earth's vain shadows flee;
In life, in death, O Lord, abide with me.

Ave Maria

Ave Maria,
Mother pure and holy,
Sorrowful, and lowly,
Blessed shall thy name
forever be
For thou art ever near us,
Thou wilt ever hear us,
Aid us Mother, aid us when
we cry to thee.

Sancta Maria,
Sancta Maria,
Maria,
Dearest Mother hear our prayer,
Take us in thy loving care,
Pray for us forever
For thy children ever pray.

Amazing Grace

Amazing Grace
How sweet the sound
To save a wretch like me
I once was lost but now I am found
Was blind but now I see.

Through many dangers,
Toils and snares
I have already come
'Tis Grace that's brought me safe this far,
And Grace will lead me home.

Amazing Grace
How sweet the sound,
To save a wretch like me
I once was lost but I am found
Was blind but now I see.

The Twenty-Third Psalm

The Lord is my shepherd; I shall not want.

He maketh me to lie down in green pastures:

He leadeth me beside the still waters.

He restoreth my soul: He leadeth me in the paths of righteousness

For His own name's sake.

Yea tho' I walk thro' the valley of the shadow of death,

I will fear no evil: for Thou art with me; Thy rod and Thy staff,

They comfort me.

Thou preparest a table before me in the presence of mine enemies:

Thou anointest my head with oil; my cup runneth over.

Surely goodness and mercy shall follow me all the days of my life:

And I will dwell in the house of the Lord for ever.

Jerusalem

And did those feet in ancient time
Walk upon England's mountains green?
And was the holy lamb of God
On England's pleasant pastures seen?
And did the countenance divine
Shine forth upon our clouded hills?
And was Jerusalem builded here
Among those dark satanic mills?

Bring me my bow of burning gold!
Bring me my arrows of desire!
Bring me my spear: O clouds unfold!
Bring me my chariot of fire!
I will not cease from mental fight;
Nor shall my sword sleep in my hand.
Till we have built Jerusalem,
In England's green and pleasant land.

Stars on Sunday
best loved readings

Prayer of
St Francis of Assisi

Lord make me a channel of thy peace

That where there is hatred,

I may bring love

That where there is wrong,

I may bring the spirit of forgiveness

That where there is discord,

I may bring harmony

That where there is error,

I may bring truth

That where there is doubts,

I may bring faith

That where there is despair,

I may bring hope

That where there are shadows,

I may bring thy light

That where there is sadness,

I may bring joy.

Lord, grant that I may seek rather to comfort,

Than to be comforted

To understand, than to be understood

To love, than to be loved

For it is by giving, that one receives,

It is by self-forgetting, that one finds

It is by forgiving, that one is forgiven

It is by dying that one awakens to eternal life.

Faith, Hope and Charity

1 Corinthians 13

Though I speak with the tongues of men and of angels, and have not charity, I am become as sounding brass, or a tinkling cymbal. And though I have the gift of prophecy, and understand all mysteries, and all knowledge; and though I have all faith, so that I could remove mountains, and have not charity I am nothing. And though I bestow all my goods to feed the poor and though I give my body to be burned, and have not charity, it profiteth me nothing. Charity suffereth long, and is kind; charity envieth not; charity vaunteth not itself, is not puffed up, Doth not behave itself unseemly, seeketh not her own, is not easily provoked, thinketh no evil; Rejoiceth not in iniquity, but rejoiceth in the truth; Beareth all things, believeth all things, hopeth all things, endureth all things. Charity never faileth: but whether there be prophecies, they shall fail; whether there be tongues, they shall cease; whether there be knowledge, it shall vanish away. For we know in part, and we prophesy in part. But when that which is perfect is come, then that which is in part shall be done away. When I was a child, I spake as a child, I understood as a child, I thought as a child; but when I became a man, I put away childish things. For now we see through a glass darkly; but then face to face: now I know in part; but then shall I know even as also I am known. And now abideth faith, hope, charity, these three; but the greatest of these is charity.

Matthew 5 v 1–16

And seeing the multitudes, he went up into
a mountain: and when he was set, his disciples came unto him: And he opened his
mouth, and taught them, saying
Blessed are the poor in spirit: for theirs is the
kingdom of heaven.
Blessed are they that mourn: for they shall
be comforted.
Blessed are the meek: for they shall inherit
the earth.
Blessed are they which do hunger and thirst
after righteousness: for they shall be filled.
Blessed are the merciful: for they shall obtain
mercy.
Blessed are the pure in heart: for they shall
see God.
Blessed are the peacemakers: for they shall
be called the children of God.
Blessed are they which are persecuted for

righteousness sake: for theirs is the kingdom of heaven.

Blessed are ye, when men shall revile you, and persecute you, and shall say all manner of evil against you falsely, for my sake. Rejoice and be exceedingly glad: for great is your reward in heaven: for so persecuted they the prophets which were before you. Ye are the salt of the earth: but if the salt have lost his savour, wherewith shall it be salted? It is thenceforth good for nothing, but to be cast out, and be trodden under foot of men. Ye are the light of the world. A city that is set on an hill cannot be hid. Neither do men light a candle, and put it under a bushel, but on a candlestick; and it giveth light unto all that are in the house. Let your light so shine before men, that they may see your good works, and glorify your Father which is in heaven.

To Everything there is a season

Ecclesiastes 3 v 1–14

To every thing there is a season, and a time to every purpose under the heaven: A time to be born, and a time to die; a time to plant, and a time to pluck up that which is planted; A time to kill, and a time to heal; a time to break down, and a time to build up; A time to weep, and a time to laugh; a time to mourn, and a time to dance; A time to cast away stones, and a time to gather stones together; a time to embrace, and a time to refrain from embracing; A time to get, and a time to lose; A time to keep, and a time to cast away; A time to rend, and a time to sew; A time to keep silence, and a time to speak; A time to love, and a time to hate; A time of war, and a time of peace. What profit hath he that worketh in that wherein he laboureth? I have seen the travail, which God hath given to the sons of men to be exercised in it. He hath made everything beautiful in his time: also He hath set the world in their heart, so that no man can find out the work that God maketh from the beginning to the end. I know that there is no good in them, but for a man to rejoice, and to do good in his life. And also that every man should eat and drink, and enjoy the good of all His labour, it is the gift of God. I know that, whatsoever God doeth, it shall be for ever: nothing can be put to it, nor any thing taken from it: God doeth it, that men should fear before him.

Desiderata

Go placidly amid the noise and haste, and remember what peace there may be in silence. As far as possible without surrender be on good terms with all persons. Speak your truth quietly and clearly; and listen to others, even the dull and ignorant; they too have their story. Keep interest in your own career, however humble; it is a real possession in the changing fortunes of time. Exercise caution in your business affairs; for the world is full of trickery. But let this not blind you to what virtue there is; many persons strive for high ideals, and everywhere life is full of heroism. Be yourself. Especially, do not feign affection. Neither be cynical about love. Take kindly the counsel of the years, gracefully surrendering the things of youth.

And do not distress yourself with imaginings. For many tears are born of fatigue and loneliness. You are a child of the universe, no less than the trees and the stars; you have a right to be here; and whether or not it is clear to you, the universe is unfolding as it should. Therefore be at peace with God, and whatever your labours and aspirations, in the noisy confusion of life keep peace with your soul. With all its sham, drudgery and broken dreams, it is still a beautiful world. Be careful. Strive to be happy.

For the Fallen
(September 1914)

With proud thanksgiving, a mother for her children,
England mourns for her dead across the sea.
Flesh of her flesh they were, spirit of her spirit,
Fallen in the cause of the free.

Solemn the drums thrill: Death august and royal
Sings sorrow up into immortal spheres.
There is music in the midst of desolation
And a glory that shines upon our tears.

They went with songs to the battle, they were young.
Straight of limb, true of eye, steady and aglow.
They were staunch to the end against odds uncounted.
They fell with their faces to the foe.

They shall grow not old, as we that are left grow old:
Age shall not weary them, nor the years condemn.
At the going down of the sun and in the morning
We will remember them.

Psalm 121

I will lift up mine eyes unto the hills: from whence
   cometh my help.

My help cometh even from the Lord: who hath
   made heaven and earth.

He will not suffer thy foot to be moved: and he
   that keepeth thee will not sleep.

Behold, he that keepeth Israel shall neither
   slumber nor sleep.

The Lord himself is thy keeper: the Lord is thy
   defence upon thy right hand;

So that the sun shall not burn thee by day: neither
   the moon by night.

The Lord shall preserve thee from all evil: yea,
   it is even he that shall keep thy soul.

The Lord shall preserve thy going out and thy
   coming in: from this time forth for evermore.

The Lord Ruleth me

He hath set me in a place of pasture: He hath brought me up on the waters of refreshment (*Psalm 22*)

In pastures green? Not always; sometimes He Who knoweth best, in kindness leadeth me In weary ways where heavy shadows be; Out of the sunshine, warm and soft and bright, Out of the sunshine into darkest night, I oft would faint with sorrow and affright. Only for this—I know He holds my hand. So whether in a green or desert land, I trust Him, though I do not understand.

And by still waters? No, not always so; Ofttime the heavy tempests round be blow, And over my soul the waves and billows go. But when the storm beats loudest and I cry Aloud for help, the Master standeth by And whispers to my soul, 'Lo! It is I.' Above the tempest wild I hear Him say: 'Beyond this darkness lies the perfect day. In every path of thine I lead the way.'

So, whether on the hilltop high and fair I dwell,
or in the sunless valley where The shadows lie—
what matter? He is there. Yea, more than this:
where'er the pathway lead, He gives to me no
helpless, broken reed. But his own Hand sufficient
for my need. So where'er He leadeth I can safely
go: And in the blest Hereafter I shall know Why,
in His Wisdom; He hath led me so.